12-0

An Insider's Account of Ohio State's
2006 Championship Season

TRIUMPH
BOOKS

This book is dedicated to the memory of Pat and Ray.
I miss them. I think they would have been proud.

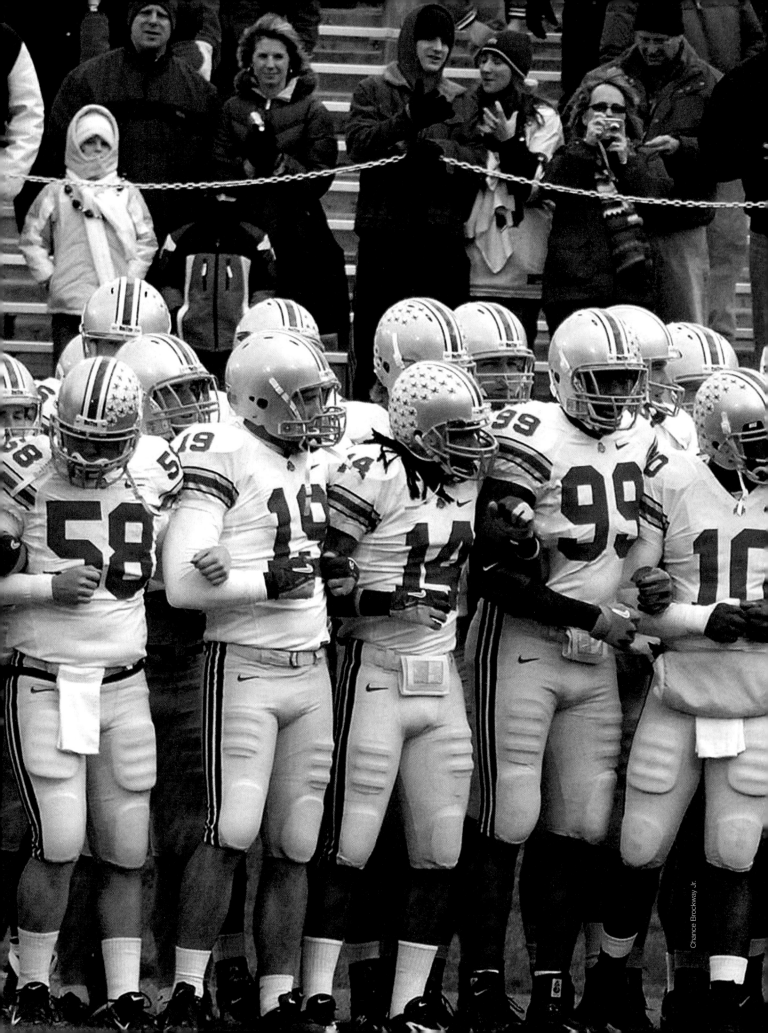

Published by Triumph Books, Chicago.

Content packaged by Mojo Media, Inc.
Editor: Joe Funk
Creative Director: Jason Hinman

This book is available in quantity at special discounts for your group or organization.
For further information, contact:

Triumph Books
542 South Dearborn Street
Suite 750
Chicago, IL 60605

Chicago, Illinois 60605
Phone: (312) 939-3330
Fax: (312) 663-3557

Printed in the United States of America

contents

Foreword

As we discussed the challenges of the 2006 football season, a common thought and singleness of purpose continued to arise. All of us, coaches and players alike, agreed that in order to become the team we wanted to be, a team that could win the Big Ten title and go on to capture the National Championship, we had to put our individual goals and agendas aside. In order to be a team, we had to become One in every way—mentally, physically and spiritually. Director of Football Operations Stan Jefferson coined the phrase "Just One Agenda", and that has been the rallying cry of the 2006 Ohio State football family.

When you have more than 100 football players and 10 full-time coaches on the team, achieving such unity is difficult at best. It is only natural to put individual goals first. But I am proud to say this team, led by a remarkable group of 19 seniors, has achieved that unity. This is a team in every sense of the word and I am enormously proud of what these young men have been able to accomplish in the classroom, on the football field and in the community.

Never, not during the 6 a.m. workouts in the winter, not in spring practice as they were developing a personality, not during the rugged two-a-days in fall camp and certainly not during the grind of a 12-week season, has this team ever lost its focus and commitment to one another.

This is the story of the 2006 Ohio State football family. The story begins shortly after our Fiesta Bowl victory over Notre Dame at the end of last year and continues through spring practice and fall camp, then relives each of our first 12 games.

We are honored to be playing in the National Championship Game and we will do our best to make sure this story has a happy ending.

Go Bucks!

–Jim Tressel
Head Football Coach
The Ohio State University

Great Expectations

"O-H" came the cry from a nearby table. "I-O" was the reply from across the room. It was a cold February night in Columbus, Ohio and the hour was late. But neither the hour, nor the snow that covered the sidewalks outside of the Rusty Bucket restaurant on Lane Avenue was enough to dampen the spirits of the mostly scarlet and gray clad clientele.

The Ohio State basketball team had just defeated Michigan State and the Buckeye fans that were in the restaurant were in a festive mood. Who could blame them? Thad Matta's young team had just made a statement to the rest of the Big Ten. No one knew it at the time, but Matta's surprising Buckeyes would go on to win the conference championship and earn an NCAA berth. Going into the season, the experts had picked the Buckeyes somewhere in the middle of the pack. As it turned out, those experts could not have been more wrong.

Brent Musburger had called the game for ESPN that night, along with Steve Lavin and Erin Andrews. Afterwards, he and I had decided to grab a quick bite to eat.

It was our first chance to get together since the Fiesta Bowl. He had been behind the microphone that night, too, as the Buckeyes rolled up 619 yards in total offense and thoroughly thrashed Notre Dame, 34-20, to close out the 2005 season with a seven-game winning streak and the No. 4 spot in the final polls.

Brent is one of those old-school announcers, capable of calling any sport, but football is his passion. So it was only natural that after we re-hashed the basketball game and speculated about the rest of the Big Ten season that our conversation eventually turned to football.

"A lot of people I have talked to have Ohio State as No. 1 going into the season," he said. "What do you think, partner?"

"Not sure we should be that high at the start," I replied. "We've lost a lot of good football players on both sides of the ball. I think by the end of the year we could be there. But going in, I'm not so sure.

"I like the way we did it in 2002, when we started out the season at No. 12 in one poll and No. 13 in the other and just worked our way up to the championship game. I think this team has that kind of potential. It's loaded on offense and young, but talented on defense. And Jim Tressel's teams always get better as the season wears on, so if we can get by (road games) Texas and Iowa early, we have a chance to be pretty good."

"Well who would be your pick as No. 1 then?" he asked.

"I guess I would say Texas as the reigning champs," I responded, thinking to myself this is only February so we have a lot of time to kick that one around. "What do you think?"

"Notre Dame, Texas, USC and West Virginia all should be pretty good," he said. "Not sure which one I would pick. The Buckeyes are right up there."

We finished our dinner and said our goodbyes. Brent headed back to the hotel (I don't envy him living out of a suitcase nine months a year) and I headed home.

Yes, it was only February, but in Columbus, Ohio football is always on your mind. And as my head hit the pillow, I

Ohio State football coach Jim Tressel holds up a Buckeyes No. 1 jersey at an April 2006 luncheon, acknowledging the fact that OSU had been the resounding preseason favorite selected by the media for the 2006-2007 season.

Members of the preseason-favorite Ohio State football team arrive for a media luncheon in Columbus in August 2006.

saw visions of Longhorns and Trojans and Leprechauns and Mountaineers and, yes Buckeyes, holding the national championship trophy aloft.

"Look up and smile. They are talking about you."

It was Bart Fox in the TV truck. I was working as Time Out Coordinator at the Big Ten men's basketball tournament in Indianapolis. Apparently there was a lull in the action because Musburger and Lavin were having a little good natured fun at my expense.

At the time I had no idea what they were discussing, but I glance toward the camera on the other side of the court and managed a sheepish smile.

"Great," I heard Bart say in my earphone. "That was a

great shot. Thanks!"

With that, I returned to the task at hand: watching some awfully good basketball from the best seat in the house. Pretty good work if you can get it. And thanks to my friend Mark Rudner at the Big Ten, I have been doing it since the inception of the Big Ten tournament.

The lady on the phone was giving me an earful.

"You guys don't understand how to promote," she said. "Ohio State should always be No. 1."

I started to say I was "OK with that," but it was hard to get a word in edgewise.

"Brent Musburger was talking about you on TV last week at the Big Ten tournament. He said you didn't think Ohio State should start out the season at No.1"

I was sinking and there was no life raft in sight. It was clear that whatever I said to her in the way of a response was going to fall on deaf ears. She had made up her mind

Sophomore offensive tackle Alex Boone answers questions from reporters on Friday, August 18, 2006 in Columbus.

that I was incapable of doing my job.

Oh, well, I thought, it is good to work at a school where the fans are passionate and at The Ohio State University, passion is a way of life when it comes to football.

"Remind me to thank Brent for that," I said to myself.

I tried to explain the value of not having a bullseye on your back all year long and that no Ohio State team had ever gone wire-to-wire, but it was easy to tell my response was falling on deaf ears.

I listened politely and thanked her for her call.

It was only March, but it was clear the expectations for the 2006 were great.

Winter conditioning came and went, so did spring practice. It was July, the football media guide was finished and the start of fall camp was right around the corner.

The unofficial start of the football season for Big Ten schools is the Big Ten Kickoff Luncheon in Chicago. The brainchild of former Big Ten Commissioner Wayne Duke, the two-day extravaganza brings together all 11 head coaches, players from each school, 350 or so members of the national media, Bowl Reps and about 1,900 fans who attend the actual luncheon on the second day.

As the old saying goes, "You can't buy that kind of publicity." Other conferences have tried to duplicate it, but with little or no luck. There is just something special about football in the Midwest.

The first Kickoff Luncheon was held in 1973. When Wayne Duke suggested it, a lot of people had their doubts. We already had a pretty good system in place for previewing the season: the Skywriters – a group of touring writers from each Big Ten city who flew via charter from campus to campus and spent a day there interviewing the head coach and players. It was 10 days of constant coverage. How could it get better than that? The Kickoff Luncheon was only two days everyone reasoned. It didn't compare. But they were wrong. And over the years, it has become the premier pre-

view event in college football.

About three weeks before this year's Luncheon, which is usually held either the last week in July or the first week in August, I received a call from Sports Illustrated. They were picking us No. 1 in their preseason issue. I was sworn to secrecy, but they wanted me to know so I could set up a photograph with Troy Smith and two of his returning starters on the offensive line, guard T.J. Downing and center Doug Datish.

Knowing firsthand the perils of the Sports Illustrated curse, I agreed to do so. It would be terrific publicity for Ohio State and the three players, especially Troy, who we were touting as a Heisman Trophy candidate.

Next came a call from USA Today. We were also their No. 1 preseason pick and they needed a quote from Ohio State coach Jim Tressel. They could meet with Coach Tressel in Chicago on the first day of the Luncheon if he could give them 10 minutes. The poll was coming out the following Friday, August 4.

Tress met with the writer on Tuesday. "We are honored," he said. "I think it shows how much respect people have for Ohio State. After all, we lost nine starters on defense and two first-round draft picks on offense.

"Of course, our goal is to be No. 1 at the end of the season. To do that we are going to have to get better each and every day through fall camp and once the season starts. That is our challenge as a football team.'

As word began to leak out that Ohio State would be No. 1, the fans in Columbus grew even more excited about the prospect of the upcoming season. Local book and novelty stores began ordering in extra merchandise, their owners thinking about a possible early retirement. And when the Associated Press had us as their top pick about a week later, it was total chaos.

That bullseye I talked about back in February was now squarely on our backs, so now the only thing to do was deal with it. ▪

Doug Datish, a senior center, responds to questions about Ohio State's first preseason No. 1 status in the AP poll since 1998.

Heisman Hype

The Heisman Trophy is the most prestigious individual award in college football. Named after former Georgia Tech Coach John W. Heisman, it was established in 1935 and is awarded each December to the "Outstanding player in college football."

Prior to the terrorist attack on New York City in 2001, the trophy was presented at the Downtown Athletic Club, a cathedral to football located on the lower east side. Now the presentation is held in mid-town Manhattan.

If you are a football fan, just walking into the "DAC" is enough to conjure up goose bumps. The building is literally steeped with tradition, or at least it was before 9-11.

In addition to a full-sized replica of the Heisman trophy and a list of past winners that occupied the center of the lobby, oil paintings of each recipient hung on the walls in the "Trophy Room."

My first visit to the DAC was in 1974 and I remember looking at those paintings and feeling a little bit like a kid in a candy shop. These were the guys who had been my childhood heroes—Army's Doc Blanchard, Glenn Davis and Pete Dawkins; Navy's Joe Bellino and Roger Staubach; Syracuse great Ernie Davis and, of course, Ohio State's own Howard "Hopalong" Cassady. I was in the presence of greatness.

Heading into the 2006 season, six Ohio State players had won the Heisman, including Archie Griffin, who in 1975 became the first two-time winner of the prestigious award. Forty years later, he is still the only person to have bookend Heismans sitting in his trophy room.

Each Ohio State winner has a story to tell.

Les Horvath was the Buckeyes' first Heisman recipient. He won the trophy in 1944. Horvath had led the Buckeyes to a 9-1 record and the national championship in 1942, but then entered dental school at OSU and hung up his cleats. Or so he thought.

After sitting out the 1943 season as he studied dentistry, Horvath was coaxed out of retirement, if you will, by first-year Ohio State coach Carroll Widdoes. Widdoes, who succeeded Paul Brown, knew that if he could find a quarterback, he had the makings of a good team. He knew, too, that Horvath was entitled to another year of eligibility because of the war.

With all the cunning of fox stocking his prey, Widdoes approached Horvath and made him an offer too good to resist: Horvath could practice on a part-time basis and the University would fly him to the away games so he wouldn't have to miss class.

Apparently football was still in his blood, because Les eventually agreed. He then went on to lead the Buckeyes to a perfect 9-0 record and the 1944 Big Ten title, setting a Big Ten rushing record in the process. At the end of the year he was selected as the Big Ten MVP and then the Heisman Trophy winner. He is the only Heisman winner who did not play the previous season.

After Les completed dental school he began his practice in Los Angeles. His wife who was not a big sports fan insisted that he get rid of many of his trophies. Les agreed, but convinced her to let him keep his Heisman because of its significance.

A couple of weeks later, Les and his wife had dinner at

Les Horvath won the Buckeyes' first Heisman Trophy back in 1944. After sitting out the '43 season to study dentistry, he was coaxed back to the gridiron by coach Carroll Widdoes.

Tom Harmon's house in Los Angeles. Tom was the 1940 Heisman winner and had his trophy prominently displayed in his trophy room.

When Les and his wife got home, she read him the riot act.

"I thought that award was special," she said. "It looks to me like everyone has one."

Vic Janowicz became the Buckeyes' second Heisman winner as a junior in 1950. Army's Doc Blanchard was the first junior to win the award, doing so in 1945. Vic was the second.

Janowicz is still regarded by many historians as the greatest all-around athlete ever to play football for the Buckeyes. In 1950, he accounted for 16 touchdowns and 875 yards in total offense and led Ohio State in scoring with 65 points.

In an 83-21 win over Iowa that year, he rushed for two touchdowns, passed for four more and converted 10 extra points.

His greatest accomplishment, however, might have come in the infamous "Snow Bowl" game against Michigan. In a driving snow storm, with the goal posts barely visible and the wind swirling, he drilled a 27-yard field goal that to this day remains one of the most memorable individual achievements in Ohio State football history.

That field goal may have been the most important play of his college career. Just as Doug Flutie sewed up the Heisman in 1984 with his "Hail Mary" touchdown pass against Boston College, Vic put the icing on the cake with his remarkable three-pointer against the Wolverines.

Following the 1950 season, Woody Hayes took over as head coach of the Buckeyes. Hayes immediately changed offenses, electing to go with the full house instead of the single-wing that his predecessor, Wes Fesler, had used. Janowicz did not play nearly as large a role in the new offense and when the Heisman Trophy results were announced he was not in the top five.

Vic never complained, but later in his career Woody would say, "If there is one thing I regret during my time at Ohio State, it is that I didn't use Vic the way I should have in 1951."

Janowicz would go on to play and excel in professional baseball and football. In 1955, he led the NFL in scoring most of the season, but lost out on the scoring title on the last day of the season.

Howard "Hopalong" Cassady was a four-year starter for the Buckeyes. The irrepressible redhead from Columbus burst on to the college scene as a freshman, coming off the bench in his first game to score three touchdowns against Indiana. From that point forward, he was a regular in Woody Hayes' lineup, playing both offense and defense.

During the time period when young Cassady was making a name for himself on the gridiron, movie star William Boyd was entertaining movie goers with a series of westerns in which he starred as Hopalong Cassidy. The last names were spelled differently, but the Buckeyes' Cassady soon had a new nickname.

"Hop" as his teammates called him, led the Buckeyes to a 10-0 record and the national championship in 1954. He won All-America honors and finished third in the Heisman balloting that year as a junior.

In 1955, Cassady ran for a then-school record 958 yards and 15 touchdowns. He again won first-team All-America honors, was named as the Associated Press Player of the Year and, to the surprise of no one, became Ohio State's third Heisman recipient.

As a boy, Cassady would sneak into Ohio Stadium to see his beloved Buckeyes play, dreaming of someday wearing the Scarlet and Gray. In 1955, he fulfilled all of his wildest dreams.

Also a star baseball player for the Buckeyes, Hop would go on to have a solid career in the National Football League, playing for Detroit, Cleveland and Philadelphia before retiring.

The Buckeyes were already on the football map before Hop entered the picture, but he made the speck a lot bigger.

Bettmann/Corbis

Vic Janowicz, regarded as perhaps the most athletic Buckeye ever, won the Heisman as a junior in 1950. His chances of a repeat performance were hindered, though, in new coach Woody Hayes's new offensive scheme in 1951.

Like Cassady, Archie Griffin was a home-grown product, playing his high school football at Columbus Eastmoor. But unlike Cassady, Griffin did not always dream of going to Ohio State. To make matters worse, after his first meeting with Ohio State coach Woody Hayes, he was sure he was headed elsewhere to continue his football career.

"He didn't talk one time about football," Arch told his dad after having dinner with Woody. "I don't think he really wants me."

Of course James Griffin knew better and before long so did Arch.

Griffin, as every Ohio State fan knows, broke into the lineup as a freshman, coming off the bench in the second game of the season to rush for 239 yards against the University of North Carolina. In doing so, he broke the existing school rushing record of 229 yards that had been set by Ollie Cline against Pittsburgh in 1945.

Who can forget that picture from after that game, showing fullback Champ Henson hugging a tearful Griffin. Archie, to this day, denies they were tears, but pictures don't lie.

Griffin would go on to become the Buckeyes all-time leading rusher with 5,589 yards on 924 carries, an average of 6.0 yards per carry. Between his sophomore and senior years, he rushed for 100 or more yards in an NCAA record 31 consecutive games.

After rushing for 1,695 yards and 12 touchdowns as a junior, Griffin won the Heisman Trophy. As he humbly introduced his family at the Heisman Dinner in the Grand Ballroom of the Waldorf-Astoria, he frequently burst into tears. This time there was no denying it.

Griffin made history in 1975 by becoming the first repeat winner of the Heisman. When asked who he wanted to bring with him to the Heisman Dinner, Griffin replied, "my entire team." He had to settle for his three co-captains – Tim Fox, Brian Baschnagel and Ken Kuhn, but his response is typical of why he was so popular with his teammates.

It was a tight race that year between Archie and Pittsburgh's Anthony Dorsett. But while Dorsett openly campaigned for the Heisman, Arch continued to credit his teammates, especially the offensive line, for his success. His humility may have been the difference in the voting.

As proud as he is of his two Heismans, Griffin will tell you to this day that the thing he is most proud of during his career at Ohio State is that he never lost to Michigan. He was 3-0-1 against "That team up North."

"Arch is the best football player I ever coached," said Hayes. "And he is a better person than he is a football player."

Today Griffin serves as the President and CEO of the Ohio State Alumni Association.

Eddie George grew up in Philadelphia. Following high school, he attended Fork Union Military Academy for a year. Recruited hard by Penn State, but as a linebacker, he chose to come to Ohio State, where Coach John Cooper had promised to give him an opportunity to play running back.

Eddie played in a reserve role his first two years, but from day one impressed the coaches with his tremendous work ethic in all that he did.

"I'm not sure I have ever seen a harder worker," said Cooper. "He's the first guy out there and the last to leave. He always wins the sprints and he spends countless hours watching film."

Eddie broke into the starting lineup as a junior and rushed for 1,442 yards and 12 touchdowns. Good, but not overwhelming numbers.

But as a senior, he rushed for a school record 1,927 yards and 24 touchdowns and also set a school mark for single-season receptions with 47 catches for 417 yards and a TD.

He rushed for 212 yards against Washington, 207 against Notre Dame and 314 against Illinois, leading the Buckeyes to 11 consecutive wins at the start of the season. His overpowering performance against a good Illinois defense locked up the Heisman.

AP/Wide World

Howard "Hopalong" Cassady had a record-setting season to win the Heisman in 1955, one year after leading the Buckeyes to the national championship as a junior.

In George and quarterback Bobby Hoying, Ohio State had two viable Heisman candidates heading into the 1995 season. But after George's 200-yard performances against Washington and Notre Dame, both of which were nationally televised, the decision was made to go with George. Not only did Eddie have the early numbers, the other leading candidates that year were all quarterbacks. With a little luck, they would split the vote and Eddie would be on most of the ballots.

Sometimes you can outthink yourself, but in this case the strategy worked.

At the start of each football season (actually the spring before), I sit down with Coach Jim Tressel and we decide which athletes to promote for All-America honors. In my opinion, and in Coach Tressel's, All-America honors and individual awards should be won through performance on the football field. But we both concede that exposure is necessary to ensure that your players are not overlooked.

How to promote has changed dramatically over the years.

My first football season at Ohio State was 1972. It was the beginning of a truly golden era of football in which the Buckeyes won four Big Ten titles, played in a still unprecedented four Rose Bowls and compiled an overall record of 40-5-1. Names like Gradishar, Hicks, Skladany, DeCree, Colzie and Griffin dotted the roster. All won first-team All-America honors, Hicks won the Outland and Lombardi Awards and finished second in the Heisman voting as a senior in 1973. Griffin, of course, remains to this day one of the most celebrated players in college football history.

Back then, there were no major promotional campaigns for players. In the days before television deregulation, teams were limited to two appearances a year. Ohio State always had two, one of which was the annual regular-season finale with Michigan. If the Buckeyes fared well in those televised games, and they usually did, they were going to get their

fair share of All-Americans.

Additonally, Woody Hayes was one of the most dominant personalities of his time. At his weekly press conferences, Woody, who could be extremely persuasive, never missed a chance to promote his players.

Griffin was already in the headlines every Sunday because of his streak of consecutive 100-yard rushing games. Hayes' effusive praise of his star running back was icing on the cake. Once Archie won the first Heisman, all the talk the following season centered around whether or not he would become the first repeat winner. Griffin responded with another outstanding year as a senior and led the Buckeyes to an unbeaten regular season. Hayes continued to praise the diminutive running back, and Griffin made football history that December by becoming the first two-time Heisman winner.

By the time Eddie George won his Heisman in 1995, promotion was in full bloom. Sports Information Directors across the country were promoting their awards candidates in a variety of ways, including mailing, billboards and gimmickry.

To help promote Eddie, we went with a series of what we believed to be creative post cards that were mailed out weekly to members of the Football Writers of America. The picture on the front changed each week, as did the information on the back, which included updated stats, any records set, and quotes from opposing coaches and players.

Eddie won the Heisman, but not because of those post cards. He ran for 1,927 yards that year and had his biggest games on national television. Still, I would like to think we helped a little.

The following year, Ohio State's best football player was junior offensive tackle Orlando Pace. Pace was probably the best football player in the country, but realistically we realized winning the Heisman would be a long shot for him.

Since offensive linemen don't have a lot of stats, we came up with a refrigerator magnet shaped like a stack of pan-

Two decades after Cassady played, one of the most beloved Buckeyes of all, Archie Griffin, gained immortal status in 1975 by being the only repeat winner in Heisman history.

cakes with Pace's name and a crown on top of it. Our not so subtle message was that Orlando Pace was king of the pancake block, a block in which the offensive lineman puts the defensive lineman across from him on his backside. And it was not an exaggeration; nobody did it better than Pace, who has gone on to become one of the dominant linemen in the NFL.

Pace did not win the Heisman but he did finish fourth. Had he stayed for his senior year, who knows?

Thankfully, the days of the gimmicky promotion seem to have gone by the wayside. Still, as I noted earlier, it is necessary to keep your athlete, or athletes, in the spotlight.

Entering this season, the general consensus among fans and media alike seemed to be that Ohio State had two legitimate Heisman contenders in quarterback Troy Smith and flanker and return specialist Ted Ginn Jr. Both were coming off strong showing the year before and both played for a team that was expected to be in the hunt for the national title. Smith had outplayed his Notre Dame counterpart, Brady Quinn, in the Fiesta Bowl, and quarterbacked the Buckeyes to consecutive wins over Michigan. Ginn, who had nine catches at Michigan and eight against the Irish in the Fiesta Bowl, was considered one of the most electrifying players in college football.

At one time, I would have argued that two candidates is one too many. The old rule of thumb was if you had two candidates you really did not have any. They would split the vote and someone else would win.

A prime example of that was in 1973 when Ohio State had three players – John Hicks, Archie Griffin and Randy Gradishar – finish in the top seven of the Heisman voting. Together, they had more votes than winner John Capaletti of Penn State.

But the University of Southern California blew that theory out of the water last year by co-promoting junior running back Reggie Bush and senior quarterback Matt Leinart. Bush won the award. Leinart, who had won it in 2004 finished third behind Bush and Texas quarterback Vince Young.

So at the conclusion of spring practice in 2006, the decision was made to promote both Troy and Teddy throughout the season. Each would get his just due and the rest would be up toe the voters.

The plan was simple. First we would try to get them as much preseason coverage as possible. That was easy. Most magazines and major publications, including Sports Illustrated, Street & Smith, Athlon, ESPN the Magazine and USA Today, came to us seeking either interviews or cover shoots.

Additionally, we would send out a preseason mailer to the 700 or so members of the Football Writers of America.

A web page would be set up for both players and a weekly teleconference would afford the national media the opportunity to call in and interview them. Associate SID Dan Wallenberg would oversee the web page and teleconference.

We would also send out another mailer the first week of November. Diana Sabau, our director of publications, came up with the idea – a card on bronze-colored stock, that featured a raised replica of the Heisman Trophy. Across the top it read: The Ohio State University. Down the sides were the names of Ohio State's six Heisman winners. No mention was made of Troy or Ted. We hoped it would be a gentle reminder at voting time.

We had a plan. Now we just had to wait and see how the season played out. Wins at Texas and at Iowa would go a long way in keeping both players in the hunt, not to mention keeping their team in the National Championship picture. ∎

During Eddie George's race to Heisman glory in 1995, he seemed to save his biggest games for the biggest stages.

Just one season removed from USC's placing two players in the top three in the Heisman voting, OSU's Troy Smith stood poised to set his sights on the trophy along with teammate Ted Ginn Jr.

Ted Ginn proved to be one of the most electrifying players in college football during the 2005 season, and he did not disappoint in his run at the trophy in 2006.

A Time for Teaching

Spring practice is a time for teaching and in many ways it is the time of the year that Jim Tressel enjoys most. Whenever the Buckeye football coach is queried as to what profession he would be in if he were not a coach, he always replies, "I would be a teacher, teaching is what I really enjoy."

As a coach, Tressel is the consummate teacher. His meetings are like classrooms and his practices are like labs in which his players put into practice what he has taught them. When practice is over, it is back to the classroom to review the day's subject matter.

Tressel's teams get better, practice-to-practice, day-to-day and game-to-game, because they understand what it takes to improve.

When spring practice opened the last week of March, Tressel knew he and his staff would need to do an extraordinary job of teaching. Nine starters from what was arguably the best defense in the nation were gone, including the magnificent linebacker trio of A.J. Hawk, Bobby Carpenter and Anthony Schlegel. On offense, center Nick Mangold and split end Santonio Holmes, both of whom would be first-round NFL Draft picks a few weeks later, needed to be replaced. Additionally, kicker Josh Huston, who tied a school record with five field goals against Texas and won all-Big Ten honors, had graduated, leaving a giant question mark in the placekicking department.

But while the losses were indeed significant, the Buckeyes have recruited well during the Tressel era and the cupboard

was certainly not bare. There was talent waiting in the wings. Tressel knew that. It was his job to develop that talent. That was his mindset as spring ball began.

Spring practice began with a bang. During the traditional "hoot and holler" drill on the first day of pads, true freshman running back Chris "Beanie" Wells flattened a veteran senior defender in a show of raw power. In the drill, an offensive player gets three chances to go ten yards. Beanie only needed one try. It was evident that the former USA Today All-American was the real deal.

The 6-1, 235-pound Wells was one of three true freshmen to enroll early. The other two, linebacker Ross Homan and defensive back Kurt Coleman , also showed well in the spring and would go on to earn playing time in the fall.

Homan was particularly impressive early and drew some favorable impressions to A.J. Hawk at a similar age.

"Ross is young but he has great instincts," said linebacker coach Luke Fickell. "If he keeps working he will help us."

The Buckeyes held their jersey scrimmage on Apr. 8, pitting the offense against the defense. The winning unit would wear the home scarlet-colored jerseys through the remainder of spring ball and into fall practice. The losers would be clad in the white away jerseys until getting a chance to redeem themselves in the fall.

Much of the media discussion leading into the spring had been about the inexperience of the defense. In stark contrast to recent years, it appeared that, early-on at least, the offense

Joe Gantz of the offensive squad is taken down by Brett Daly during the 2006 Ohio State spring scrimmage between the two units.

More than 63,000 Buckeye fans fill Ohio Stadium for the annual spring football scrimmage on April 22, 2006.

would have to carry the defense.

On this day, the defense was having none of that. Jim Heacock's young, but undeniably talented, and surprisingly fast, defensive unit forced five turnovers and came away with a 69-68 victory, using a unique scoring system first put together by Jim Tressel's father, the late Lee Tressel.

Several young players stood out on the defensive side of the ball, including, but not limited to, Ross Homan (LB), Andre Amos (CB), Anderson Russell (S), Todd Denlinger (DT), Lawrence Wilson (DE) and James Laurinaitis (LB).

"You can tell these young guys want to be good and uphold the tradition of excellent Ohio State defense," said Tressel, who down deep inside probably did not mind the outcome. "This will help their confidence."

The defense won the scarlet jerseys even though tackle Quinn Pitcock, one of just two returning starters on that side of the ball, did not play. Pitcock would sit out the entire spring recovering from minor shoulder surgery.

The offense was without two of its top offensive linemen, right tackle Kirk Barton and Doug Datish, who after starting at guard in 2004 and guard in 2005 would move to center in the fall of 2006 with the unenviable task of replacing All-America center Nick Mangold.

"But Troy Smith would not use that as an excuse.

"We got our butts whipped and I don't like that feeling whether it is in a practice or a scrimmage," he said.

The scrimmage came down to a 58-yard field goal attempt by Ryan Pretorius on the final play of the game. When the defense blocked the kick, it was worth one point for the stop and broke a 68-all tie.

The kicking game has always played an important role in the success of Tressel's teams, both in his 15 years at Youngstown State where he won four Division 1-AA national championships, and at Ohio State, where in just his second year he captured the 2002 national championship.

Tressel, who calls "the punt the most important play in football," has had a remarkable string of kickers since coming to Ohio State.

Mike Nugent was a three-year starter at placekicker during the 2002, 2003 and 2004 seasons and won first-team All-American honors in '02 and again in '04. In the latter season he also won the Lou Groza Award as the nation's top

Jamario O'Neal (3) pulls down an interception in front of Albert Dukes during OSU's scrimmage on April 22, 2006.

placekicker. In 2005, Mike Nugent took over Nugent's duties and the Buckeyes never missed a beat.

In the punting department, Andy Groom was a first-team All-America pick in 2002 as was B. J. Sander the following year. Sander also became the school's first Ray Guy Award winner in 2003.

With A. J. Trapasso returning in 2006, the Buckeyes' punting game was in good hands, but placekicking was another story.

The job would go to either Ryan Pretorius, a 27-year-old sophomore from Durban, South Africa, or Aaron Pettrey, a redshirt freshman from Raceland, Ky. Both were untested, although, Pretorius had appeared in one game in 2005.

Tressel hoped to get an answer in the kick scrimmage, but when Pretorius hit 6 of 7 tries and Pettrey drilled a 60-yarder to give the Gray team a 28-27 win, he headed into the fall still looking for a clear-cut No. 1.

"Looks like we have a pretty good battle going on," he said. "We will just have to wait until the fall and see what happens."

Football is a violent game. Over the years, players have gotten, bigger, stronger and faster. Sometimes the collisions on the field are unnerving.

Ohio State has been fortunate never to have a fatality in either a practice or a game. And up until this spring, the Buckeyes had never had a serious neck or spinal cord injury.

That changed on April 14 during a scrimmage in Ohio Stadium on Easter weekend.

Walk-on Tyson Gentry, who made the squad as a punter and for the first time this spring was also working at wide receiver, was running a square-in when he was tackled by freshman defensive back Kurt Coleman. The hit was clean and was not one of those bone-jarring tackles that make fans cringe.

But when the two players hit the ground, Tyson was completely motionless. Everyone in the stadium, the coaches, the players, the doctors and trainers and the family mem-

bers in the stands, including his parents, Bob and Gloria Gentry, could tell right away it was serious.

As the team doctors and his parents hurried to his side, the training staff called 911 for transportation.

All the while there was an eerie hush in the stadium. All of us were thinking, come on Tyson, just move something.

But while Tyson was conscious and talking the entire time, there was no movement.

Once the ambulance left for the Ohio State medical center, coach Jim Tressel called the team together. After a brief prayer for Tyson and his family, the coach cancelled practice and sent the team home for the Easter holiday.

Tressel immediately headed to the hospital along with several members of the team.

Gentry suffered a fracture of the C4 vertebra. He had surgery that night and again the next day to fuse the vertebra. Then the long process of rehabilitation began as he moved into Dodd Hall to start his physical therapy.

The outpouring of support from Ohio State fans, and really people everywhere, was overwhelming.

Tyson made his first public appearance at the Ohio State Scholar-Athlete Dinner in late May. When Director of Athletics Eugene Smith introduced him, he received a standing ovation. There was not a dry eye in the room.

Through hard work and the love and faith of his family, Tyson has made steady progress, gradually regaining movement in the upper body. His lower body has been slower to respond, but he is making progress.

As a tribute to their fallen teammate, the Buckeyes have a No. 24 decal on their helmets.

There is an old saying that bad things happen in threes.

On the evening of May 26, I received a phone call from Jim Bollman, our offensive coordinator.

"Hey Bolls, what's up?" I asked.

"I wanted to give you a call and let you know what was happening with me just in case you didn't know," he said.

Ohio State kicker Ryan Pretorious drills a field goal to bolster the offensive unit during the Buckeyes' intrasquad spring game. Pretorious's last-second attempt later in the game was blocked to give the defense a 1-point win under Coach Tressel's special scoring format.

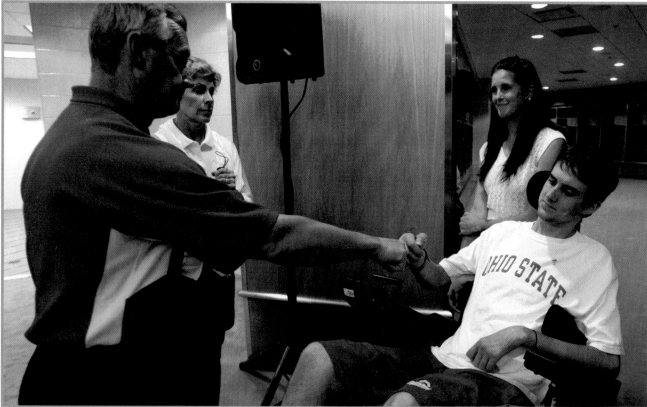

Coach Tressel bumps knuckles with Tyson Gentry three and a half months after Gentry suffered a broken neck during spring practices.

"I have no idea what you are talking about," I responded.

"Well, I am over here at University Hospitals and I am going to have open heart surgery tomorrow," he explained. "I was on the road recruiting earlier in the week and just didn't feel good, so I came home and saw the doctor. They did some preliminary tests and decided to do the surgery sooner rather than later. So we are doing it tomorrow."

Knowing Bolls as I do, he had to be feeling really bad to come home.

"Good luck," I said. "Tell Terry [his wife] not to worry, you are too ornery to have anything bad happen."

As we all hoped, Bolls' surgery did go well and he was

home later that week. He would spend the next six weeks there recovering and adapting to a new lifestyle. When fall camp opened the first week of August, Bolls, forty pounds slimmer but just as cantankerous, was back on the job.

About three weeks after the Bollman surgery, quarterbacks coach Joe Daniels experienced some discomfort in his chest while at the office. A visit to the emergency room confirmed that he had suffered a mild heart attack.

Doctors determined it would not be necessary to do open heart surgery. They could solve the problem with stints. That was the good news.

Unfortunately, bad news followed. While doing some follow-up testing, doctors discovered a malignant tumor near Joe's kidney. Joe was stunned. He had been feeling fine and had no idea anything was wrong.

Joe immediately began treatment. Like Bolls, he spent the

Ohio State coaches Joe Daniels (left) and Jim Bollman confer on the sidelines during a practice on August 7, 2006 in Columbus. Both coaches suffered serious medical setbacks in the offseason but found their way back to the sidelines for the start of the season.

last half of June and all of July at home getting stronger. But when practice opened he was right there with the quarterbacks ready to go. Amazingly, he has not missed a practice or a meeting because of his illness.

One thing for sure, if the Ohio State Medical Center or the James Cancer Hospital ever needs an endorsement, the Ohio State football family will be happy to provide it.

As spring practice progressed, it was obvious to those close to the program that this could be a very good football team. Yes, it was young, but the offense was deep and explosive and the defense was athletic and maybe faster that a year ago. It would hold up its end of the bargain.

Troy Smith was particularly impressive. The Buckeye quarterback had a presence about him that let you know he was in complete command. He could always make all the throws, now he was thirsting to know everything he could about the offense and that thirst was paying off.

With Smith at the helm, protected by a veteran offensive line, and blessed with talent and depth at both receiver and running back, this could be one of the most explosive offenses in Ohio State history.

On the other side of the ball, even though tackle Quinn Pitcock was sitting out the spring with a shoulder injury, the defensive line showed loads of promise. David Patterson, the other returning starter would move from end to tackle, giving the Buckeyes one of the best inside tandems in college football. Todd Denlinger and Joel Penton would provide solid depth at tackle, and Jay Richardson, Lawrence Wilson and Vernon Gholston were three very capable ends.

James Laurinaits and Ross Homan headed up a group of promising linebackers that included Curtiss Terry, Marcus Freeman, John Kerr and junior college All-America transfer Larry Grant. If need be, it could be linebacker by committee.

Senior safety Brandon Mitchell and sophomore cornerback Malcolm Jenkins headed up a secondary that also included senior Antonio Smith, sophomore Nick Patterson and a parcel of redshirt freshman, including Anderson Russell, Andre Amos and Donald Washington.

The public got its first look at the team on April 22 at the annual Scarlet and Gray spring game. The spring game routinely attracts numbers in excess of 30,000, but on this day that figure would more than double with an announced crowd of 63,649, not counting children six-and-under. And the game was broadcast by WBNS radio and televised locally and around the state by WBNS-TV and the Ohio News Network.

The game itself was won by the Scarlet team as Smith directed a nine-play, 80-yard touchdown drive on his team's opening possession. Smith completed four passes on the march for 68 yards. Erik Haw, who has since transferred, scored the only touchdown of the day on a four-yard run.

The Scarlet team scored five points in the second quarter on a safety and a 38-yard field goal by Ryan Pretorius to complete the scoring.

Freshman Chris "Beanie" Wells rushed for 48 yards for the Scarlet and Maurice Wells rushed for 34 yards to lead the Gray squad.

Brian Hartline had seven receptions for 88 yards for the Scarlet to lead all receivers. Roy Hall had five catches for 66 yards for the Gray.

The Scarlet took a 9-0 lead when Todd Denlinger, tackled Maurice Wells in the end zone and made it 12-0 on the three-pointer by Pretorius.

Spring Practice was over.

"We have had a good winter conditioning program and a good spring," said Tressel, addressing the media after the spring game. "What is most important now is how hard our players work during the summer leading up to fall camp.

Next up: The Big Ten Kickoff Luncheon in Chicago on Aug. 1-2, followed by the players reporting to fall camp on Aug. 7.

The season was getting closer. ∎

Ohio State quarterback Troy Smith was particularly impressive when the Buckeyes resumed practices in the summer, poised to lead his team to the national championship game.

The Season Begins
Ohio State 35, Northern Illinois 12

Finally all the hype was over. It was game week and you could see the excitement in the eyes of the players and coaches alike. After three weeks of fall camp, the players were anxious to hit someone other than their own teammates. The coaches, head coach Jim Tressel included, were anxious to see their product perform on the field. And the fans, oh the fans, they were ready for their beloved Buckeyes to begin the quest for the Holy Grail, the national championship. Everyone had a little bit more pep in their step!

As expected, much of the early buzz about the Buckeyes, especially on talk radio, speculated that the offense with all its many weapons would have to carry the load early while the young defense matured and learned the ropes.

"I have never been around a team with so many guys capable of making big plays," conceded offensive coordinator Jim Bollman. "And the offensive line is the deepest it has been in my six years here." From the normally tight-lipped Bollman that was hearty praise indeed.

Defensive coordinator Jim Heacock also made an interesting observation: "We have a lot of holes to fill, but one thing that has impressed me about this bunch right from the start is the great effort they give. As a coach, that makes you feel good."

When asked to asses his team heading into the opener, Tressel replied, "In reality, we are probably not as good on offense or as bad on defense as everyone thinks."

One of the things that had the Buckeye coach excited was the senior class. There are 17 seniors on the 2006 roster, 16 of which are fifth-year players.

"In order for us to be a great team, our seniors will need to have a great year," declared Tressel. "We have a veteran group of seniors who will be great leaders."

Northern Illinois was the opening opponent. The Huskies, under the direction of Joe Novak, were a veteran team that averaged 32.4 points and 444.1 yards per game in 2005. Among their returnees was tailback Garrett Wolfe, a preseason All-American and the nation's leading returning rusher. In games against Michigan and Northwestern last year, the diminutive Wolfe amassed 393 yards rushing and scored four touchdowns.

Nor were the Huskies likely to be intimidated by playing in front of 102,000 scarlet and gray-clad fans into Ohio Stadium. They are accustomed to playing the Big Boys. In 2003, they knocked off Iowa State, Alabama and Maryland, all on the road, on the way to a 10-2 record.

"This is a good football team and will certainly be a good test for our young defense," Tressel warned. "I know this, we better be prepared for Garrett Wolfe because he is coming after you."

This would be the seventh time that Ohio State had opened the season as No. 1 in the Associated Press poll. Although the Buckeyes have won seven national championships, no Ohio State team has ever gone wire-to-wire. They hoped to change that in 2006.

The game against Northern Illinois was televised by ABC and did not kickoff until 3:30 p.m. in Ohio Stadium. Probably a good thing since it had rained the night before

Maurice Wells finds open field in Ohio State's win over Northern Illinois.

Ted Ginn Jr. (7) and Anthony Gonzalez (11) celebrate a touchdown against Northern Illinois in the Buckeyes' season opener. Ginn's two TD receptions and Gonzalez's lone one helped put OSU up 21-0 after their first three possessions.

and the field had been covered. The late kickoff gave the field a little time to air out.

Once the Buckeyes took the field, however, they gave Northern Illinois no time to get ready.

With quarterback Troy Smith seemingly in mid-season form, OSU scored on its first four possessions to jump out to a 28-0 lead.

Smith capped off the first three drives with touchdown passes—the first two to Ted Ginn Jr. and the third to Anthony Gonzalez. Freshman Chris Wells made it 28-0 on an 8-yard run early in the second period and the Buckeyes led 28-3 at the half.

The halftime statistics told the story. Ohio State had 297 yards in total offense, Northern Illinois had 176.

Smith had hit 13 of his 17 passes for 208 yards and the three scores, while tailback Antonio Pittman had rushed for

69 yards on 11 carries, 10 more yards than the Huskies' Wolfe.

The Buckeyes' young and inexperienced defense had missed a few tackles, perhaps due to nervousness more than anything else, but had recorded an interception and allowed NIU to convert just one-of-seven third-down situations. And they had not given up a touchdown. That had to be a confidence builder.

Northern Illinois tallied another field goal in the third quarter, but Pittman's 1-yard run at the start of the fourth increased the OSU lead to 35-6.

The Huskies lone touchdown of the day came on a four-yard pass from Phil Horvath to Wolfe with 10:27 to play. The try for two was no good and the Buckeyes wound up with a convincing 35-12 victory.

Smith completed 18-of-25 passes for 297 yards. Ginn had four receptions for 123 yards and Gonzalez four for 53. Pittman topped the 100-yard mark with 111 on 19 carries. The Buckeyes finished with 488 yards of total offense.

Wolfe was every bit as good as advertised, rushing for 176 yards on 26 carries for the Huskies who totaled 343 yards.

There was still plenty of room for improvement on both sides of the ball, but the Buckeyes had passed their first test.

Now, it was on to Austin and the game everyone had been talking about since last January. ■

Northern Illinois vs #1 Ohio State (Sep 2, 2006 at Columbus, Ohio)

Score by Quarters	1	2	3	4	Score	
Northern Illinois	0	3	3	6	12	Record: (0-1)
Ohio State	21	7	0	7	35	Record: (1-0)

Ray Small gains extra yardage after a reception from quarterback Troy Smith during OSU's 2006 season opener.

Showdown Time
Ohio State 24, Texas 7

This was the game that Ohio State fans had been waiting for, an opportunity to repay the Longhorns for their 25-22 upset of the Buckeyes last year in Columbus.

Buoyed by that victory in front of a record crowd of 105,565 in Ohio Stadium, Texas would go on to win the 2005 National Championship, posting a 13-0 record and defeating Southern Cal, 41-38, in the title game at the Rose Bowl. The Buckeyes would finish at 10-2 and a very solid No. 4 in the final polls. But at the end of the year most experts agreed, Texas and Ohio State were the two best teams in college football.

Texas returned 14 starters, seven on each side of the ball. But the Longhorns were minus All-America quarterback Vince Young, who had all but single-handedly upended USC in the championship game. Much to the chagrin of Texas coach Mack Brown, the multi-talented Young had chosen to forgo his senior year and enter the NFL Draft. But even without Young, the No. 2 Longhorns had opened the 2006 season with a 56-7 thrashing of North Texas to extend their winning streak to an impressive 21 straight. They also had won 18 of their last 19 games in Darrell K. Royal-Texas Memorial Stadium and had scored 40 or more in 12 consecutive regular-season games.

The Buckeyes young defense would have its hands full. Hopefully, the OSU offense, with its vast arsenal of weaponry, would be the difference.

This would be the earliest regular-season meeting ever between a No. 1 and No. 2 team. History was on Ohio State's side. The Buckeyes were 2-0 all-time in such games, defeating No. 1 USC in the 1969 Rose Bowl and No. 1 Miami in the 2003 Tostitos Fiesta Bowl.

Not that this game needed any more hype, but just for good measure it was being televised in prime time by ABC and College GameDay would be in the house to help rev up the excitement.

The Buckeyes had been allotted 4,000 tickets. They easily could have sold ten times as many. Any Texas fan with tickets in hand and without a real passion to see the Longhorns play, could make out quite handsomely.

During the week, the national media focused most of its attention on OSU quarterback Troy Smith, who like Young was as adept at beating a team with his legs as he was with his cannon of a right arm. Like Young, Smith also wore jersey No. 10.

"What separates Troy from some of the other quarterbacks I have been around, and Vince Young had it too, is his command on the field. The players know he is in charge and is going to make a play when we need it," said Tressel of his senior signal caller.

The ABC crew of Brent Musburger, Bob Davie and Lisa Salters arrived in Austin on Thursday. The fourth member of their team, Kirk Herbstreit, along with most of the national media, came to town Friday, anxious to avail themselves of some Texas hospitality and some pretty good food, too.

Musburger was gracious enough to take time out of his tightly scripted schedule to meet with a group of Ohio State

Ohio State quarterback Troy Smith looks for an open receiver during the Buckeyes' payback win over Texas on September 9, 2006.

Buckeyes running back Antonio Pittman bowls through two Texas defenders in first-quarter action against Texas.

Usually the latter session involves a brief look-see after which the team hops back on the busses and returns to the hotel. This one took a bit longer as Tressel allowed his players to familiarize themselves with the stadium, the field and the lights. He also wanted them to get used to the heat. Temperatures in Austin had hovered in the 100s for the past few weeks, and while the players had been continually hydrating themselves since the first day of fall camp, there really is no substitute for the real thing.

Saturday's on the road always drag out, especially when it is a night game. The coaches keep the players occupied with unit meetings and individual film study leading up to the pre-game meal which is always four hours before the game.

The players also have time to watch other games that might be on and spend some time with their family members.

The team and its entourage left for the stadium just after 4:30 p.m. The police escort helped the busses wind their way through the crowded streets and parking lots. On the way in, they passed the GameDay set, where earlier in the day Lee Corso had donned a 10-gallon hat signifying that he was picking the Longhorns over the Buckeyes.

As it turned out the temperature at game time was 85 and bearable, especially once the sun went down. The atmosphere was electric, not as much so in a game in Ohio Stadium but nonetheless electric. Celebrities were everywhere: LeBron James and Eddie George were on the Ohio State sideline and Matthew McConaughey, a native Texan, was cheering for the Longhorns from a private suite.

Once the game started, the two teams traded punches like a couple of heavyweight contenders early on, each looking

supporters on Friday morning at the team hotel. During his 20-minute presentation, he threw in a nice little anecdote about Troy Smith, who attended a summer camp sponsored by EA Sports and was a favorite of many of the younger campers because of the time he took with each of them.

"As a young man, Troy made a very favorable impression," said Musburger. "That tells you a little bit about the Ohio State program under the direction of Jim Tressel."

The team landed in Austin early Friday afternoon. After getting checked in and eating the traditional Friday night meal, which always includes pecan rolls from the OSU Golf Course (a tradition that dates back to Woody Hayes), they headed off to Memorial Stadium for a walk-through.

OSU linebacker James Laurinaitis knocks the ball loose from Texas wideout Selvin Young, causing a fumble in the Buckeyes' early season win over the Longhorns.

for the other's underbelly.

Both missed early scoring chances.

Ohio State took the opening kickoff and moved from its own 20 to the Texas 8, but missed a 28-yard field goal attempt. On the second play of that drive, Smith hit Ted Ginn Jr. on a crossing route and 46 yards later the Buckeyes had the ball on Texas 31. Ginn had not been much of a factor in last year's game, but that would not be the case this time around.

Texas punted on its first possession, but after forcing an Ohio State punt, the Longhorns took over at their own 20 and moved down the field behind the running of Jamaal Charles and Selvin Young, two talented backs with speed and the ability to make tacklers miss. After a pass interference call, Texas was knocking on the door at the OSU 7. That's when sophomore linebacker James Laurinaitis stripped the ball from Texas receiver Billy Pittman and cornerback Donald Washington scooped it up at the 2 and returned it 48 yards to midfield. The Buckeyes' young defense had stepped up.

Going into the game Tressel had planned to play a lot of players. There were two reasons for that. First, he wanted to see how his young players would do against quality competition. Second, he wanted to keep his players fresh in the Texas heat.

Part of that substitution plan involved playing the second-team offensive line on the third series of the game. So after Washington's return, out trotted center Tyler Whaley, guards Kyle Mitchum and Ben Person and tackles John Skinner and Tim Schaffer.

With that unlikely fivesome leading the way, the Buckeyes marched smartly down the field and took a 7-0 lead on a 14-yard pass from Smith to Anthony Gonzalez. The 50-yard drive had taken just five plays. Gonzalez, who would become one of the major stories of the night, had three receptions on the drive, including a 26-yarder on the first play that put the Longhorns on their heels.

Texas tied the score at 7-7 with 1:55 to go in the half on a two-yard pass from McCoy to Pittman. It was the longest drive of the night by either team, covering 78 yards in 13 plays.

The Buckeyes then ran their two-minute drill to perfection as Smith hit four consecutive passes to move the ball from the OSU 34 to the Texas 29 with 22 seconds remaining in the half. Gonzalez had caught two of those passes and already had seven receptions for 122 yards and there was still a half to play. The Longhorns had been concentrating on stopping Ginn. In the process they forgot about the other half of the Buckeyes' talented receiving tandem.

Ohio State took a timeout to set up a play. When the Buckeyes broke the huddle, Ginn, on the left side, had single coverage. The crowd saw it and began to buzz. Smith and Ginn also recognized it and made eye contact.

Ginn was two steps, and then some, past his lone defender when the perfectly thrown spiral landed softly in his hands. The Buckeyes led 14-7 with 16 seconds to play in the half. The Texas crowd stared at the gigantic scoreboard in disbelief.

By halftime, Smith had completed 13-of-19 passes for 219 yards and the two touchdowns and the Buckeyes had rolled up 258 yards in total offense. The OSU defense had given up 191 yards, but only one touchdown and had come up with a key turnover.

Sophomore punter A. J. Trapasso kept the Longhorns pinned deep in their own territory with punts of 59, 56 and 41 yards.

But Texas would get the ball to open the second half and the Longhorns were just a play away from tying the score. The OSU defense would have to sustain.

Texas ran the ball two straight times and picked up the first down. On the next play, McCoy threw over the middle, but into the waiting hands of Laurinaitis, who returned the ball 25 yards to the Texas 21. It was the first career interception for Laurinaitis.

Wide receiver Anthony Gonzalez (left) celebrates his 12-yard TD reception from quarterback Troy Smith (right) during the Buckeyes' win over Texas in Austin.

AP/Wide World

Coach Tressel joins in a chorus of the Buckeyes' school song after the final whistle blew in Austin, Texas.

ning tailback Antonio Pittman. Pittman carried the ball five times on the drive and also had a reception. Smith completed four-of-five passes.

Ohio State 24, Texas 7! There would be no more scoring.

Smith certainly did nothing to damage his Heisman Trophy chances, completing 17 of 26 passes for 269 yards and the two scores. He was in total command of the game from start to finish, almost surgically dissecting the Texas secondary.

Gonzalez had a career day with eight receptions for 142 yards and Ginn had five catches for 97. Pittman chipped in with 74 yards on 14 carries. The Buckeyes simply had too much firepower.

The Texas defense forced the Buckeyes to settle for a field goal, but OSU led 17-7 after Aaron Pettrey's 31-yard kick and had a little breathing room.

Ohio State led by 10 heading into the fourth quarter and was clearly outplaying the second-ranked Longhorns.

The only other scoring opportunity for Texas came with just over eight minutes to play, but Greg Johnson's 45-yard field goal attempt was wide to the right.

Ohio State then put the game away with a 10-play, 72-yard drive that culminated with a 2-yard run by hard-run-

Trapasso kept up his stellar play in the second half and wound up averaging 50.8 yards per kick on six punts, the third best single-game average in OSU history.

Following the game, Ohio State would be chosen as the National Team of the Week, while Laurinaitis, who finished his night's work with 13 tackles, an interception, a tackle-for-loss and two forced fumbles, was chosen as the Walter Camp, Sporting News and Nagurski National Player of the week.

The Buckeyes had snapped the Longhorns' 21-game winning streak and had certainly solidified themselves as the No. 1 team in the nation. The team got home shortly after 4 a.m., but no one seemed to mind. ■

#1 Ohio State vs #2 Texas (Sep 09, 2006 at Austin, Texas)

Score by Quarters	1	2	3	4	Score	
Ohio State	7	7	3	7	24	Record: (2-0)
Texas	0	7	0	0	7	Record: (1-1)

Quarterback Troy Smith and quarterbacks coach Joe Daniels celebrate the Buckeyes' 24-7 win over Texas in the much-anticipated matchup in Austin, Texas.

Don't Believe Your Press Clippings
Ohio State 37, Cincinnati 7

Letdown is a seven-letter word sure to give coaches gray hair. There is nothing worse than coming off a big win one week and stumbling the next against a supposedly inferior opponent.

But while Jim Tressel does have a few more gray locks than he did when he took the Ohio State job six years ago, they are not the result of his teams overlooking an upcoming opponent.

On the contrary, Tressel has a remarkable knack of keeping his players focused on the task at hand. In fact, heading into this year, his Ohio State teams owned a combined record of 19-5 the week after playing a ranked team in-season.

And while Ohio State was coming off a convincing road win at then-No. 2 Texas, the players knew better than to overlook their upcoming meeting with the University of Cincinnati on Saturday, not with former Buckeye assistant coach Mark Dantonio now calling the shots for the Bearcats.

Dantonio had been a favorite of the OSU players during his three seasons (2001-03) as the Buckeyes' defensive coordinator. They respected him immensely as a coach and knew he would have his team ready to play when it came to Columbus.

Tressel and Dantonio were good friends. They had gotten to know one another in 1983 and '84 while on Earle Bruce's staff at Ohio State. At the time, Tressel coached the quarterbacks and wide receivers, and Dantonio served as a gradu-ate assistant. When Tressel left Ohio State to become the head coach at Youngstown State in 1986, he hired Dantonio on a full-time basis. The two spent five very successful years together at YSU.

Dantonio coached at Kansas and Michigan State after leaving Youngstown. He was defensive coordinator for Michigan State in 1998 when the Spartans upset the No. 1 ranked Buckeyes in Ohio Stadium.

This would be Dantonio's second visit to Columbus since leaving the Buckeyes. He brought the Bearcats to Ohio Stadium in 2004 in his first game as a head coach. The Buckeyes won that encounter, owned a commanding 12-2 lead in the series and had not lost to the Bearcats since 1897. Additionally, OSU had won all seven games played in Columbus. But a quick look at the game films from 2002 would remind anyone who had forgotten that the Buckeyes were fortunate to escape Paul Brown Stadium with a 23-19 win in their national championship year.

Tressel was not about to let his team get big head, this or any other week. Still, this was the kind of game he does not enjoy. Dantonio and his wife and children are like family to Tressel. To make matters worse, his nephew, Mike Tressel, coaches the Bearcats linebackers and special teams and is the son of Dick Tressel, who coaches the OSU running backs.

Better to get this one over with and get on to Big Ten play.

As Tressel had expected, Cincinnati was not about to roll

Troy Smith kept his Heisman hopes, and the Buckeyes' memorable season, on course with a 21-for-30, 203-yard performance including two TD throws to Ted Ginn Jr. against Cincinnati.

Ohio State cornerback Antonio Smith puts a hit on a Cincinnati ballcarrier during the Buckeyes' victory.

over in awe of the Buckeyes.

After Ohio State took a 3-0 lead on a 47-yard field goal by Aaron Pettrey, the Bearcats responded with a five-play, 80-yard drive to take a 7-3 lead with 6:36 to play in the first quarter. It was the first time this year that the Buckeyes had trailed.

Quarterback Dustin Grutza completed all three of his passes on the drive, including a 22-yard scoring strike to Jared Martin. On the play that preceded the touchdown, he eluded the on-coming OSU rush and picked up 23 yards before being run out of bounds.

It was still 7-3 at the end of the first quarter. Imagine what college football fans everywhere were thinking as that score flashed on their televisions.

But Pettrey added a second field goal early in the second quarter to cut the deficit to 7-6 and the Buckeyes took the lead for good with three minutes to play in the half when quarterback Troy Smith and flanker Ted Ginn Jr. hooked up on a 12-yard pass.

Smith hit all six of his passes on the go-ahead drive, including a 33-yard toss to Anthony Gonzalez that put the ball on the Cincinnati 6. After a holding penalty moved the ball back to the 17, tailback Antonio Pittman picked up five yards. On second-and-goal from the 12, Smith found Ginn on a crossing route and OSU was on top 13-7 at the half.

The Buckeyes punted on their first possession of the second half. On their second, they turned to Pittman, who provided the spark that was necessary by picking up 13, 6, 8 and 11 yards on four consecutive carries as the Buckeyes marched from their own 40 to the UC 22. Two plays later, Smith and Ginn hooked up on their second touchdown of the day, this time from nine-yards away. Suddenly Ohio State was in total command.

Pittman was the star of the game, finishing the day with 155 yards on 16 carries, an average of 9.7 yards per attempt. He had 103 of those yards after intermission, including a 48-yard touchdown that run extended the Buckeyes lead to 27-7 with just under 10 minutes remaining.

On Pittman's long run, Ginn leveled an unsuspecting Bearcat with a nasty block just before the Buckeye tailback crossed the goal line.

Ginn and Gonzalez each had five receptions as OSU's four quarterbacks combined to hit 11 different receivers.

Defensive tackle Quinn Pitcock had a career day for the defense, recording a personal-high three sacks and narrowly missing two more. Pitcock, who had one sack all of last year, was fast becoming one of the best d-linemen in the country.

After the game, Tressel said, "I can't imagine anyone with a pair of better inside players than Quinn Pitcock and David Patterson."

The Buckeyes had nine tackles-for-loss, eight of which were sacks. They also picked off three interceptions – one each by James Laurinaitis, Malcolm Jenkins and Anderson Russell. It was the second interception in as many games for Laurinaitis, the surprising sophomore from Minnesota.

"I think Cincinnati was the best team we have played this year in terms of being ready to play against us," said OSU offensive guard T. J. Downing after the game. "Their front four is very good and they had our receivers pretty well blanketed the first half. They threw some thing at us we hadn't seen before, but we knew Coach Dantonio would come up with something to keep us off balance."

Tressel and Dantonio shook hands after the game and headed to their respective locker rooms, secure in the knowledge that the two schools don't meet again until 2012. ■

Cincinnati vs #1 Ohio State (Sep 16, 2006 at Columbus, Ohio)

Score by Quarters	1	2	3	4	Score	
Cincinnati	7	0	0	0	7	Record: (1-2)
Ohio State	3	10	7	17	37	Record: (3-0)

Defensive End Jay Richardson (99) and the Buckeyes defense kept the Bearcats in check when they had to during their third win of the season.

Big Ten Time
Ohio State 28, Penn State 6

The Woody Hayes Athletics Center is adorned with regalia of all types, including replicas of Ohio State's six Heisman Trophies and the 2002 National Championship Trophy.

There are also numerous photographs of former Buckeye greats and award winners throughout the building, including the likes of Archie Griffin, Eddie George, Terry Glenn, Orlando Pace and Antoine Winfield just to name a few.

But in the team meeting room, where the coaches and players huddle as a unit, there are only two team pictures on the walls – those of the 2002 National Championship team and the 1984 Big Ten championship team, the last Buckeye squad to win an outright Big Ten title.

"Our goal every year is to win the Big Ten title outright," said quarterback Troy Smith. "Coach Tressel tells us all the time if you want to have your picture up as Big Ten champions, then you need to win it outright."

The Buckeyes have come close in two of Tressel's first five years at Ohio State. They posted a perfect 8-0 record on the way to an unblemished 14-0 mark and the national championship in 2002. But Iowa also finished at 8-0 that year, so the two teams were forced to share the crown.

Last year, Ohio State and Penn State had identical 7-1 conference records. The Buckeyes lost to the Nittany Lions, 17-10, in a game that went down to the wire in State College. Penn State dropped a last-second 27-25 decision at Michigan for its only loss of the season.

"If you want to be assured of winning the Big Ten outright, then you better win all your games," said Tressel.

"That is our No.1 goal every year. If you can do that, everything else will take care of itself."

Since that loss to Penn State, the Buckeyes had reeled off 10 consecutive victories, including six straight Big Ten games, and were 3-0 heading into this year's match-up. Penn State was 2-1, losing at Notre Dame in week two of the season. Like the Buckeyes, Penn State had lost a number of players to graduation, including talented quarterback Michael Robinson, who was the piston that kept the Nittany Lions hitting on all cylinders in 2005.

Judging by his comments after the Cincinnati game, Tressel, and his players, were eager to get going in league play.

"We are anxious for the Big Ten to start and I think our play against Cincinnati showed that at times," he said.

But the coach also noted, "From here on out it is going to get tougher, so we need to keep getting better as a team."

The excitement of beginning league play was augmented by the start of classes on Wednesday. Ohio State is on quarters academically and it can be pretty quiet on campus between sessions, so it was nice for the players to have the students back and involved.

Of course the first day of classes is always a little hectic, especially for the freshmen who all of a sudden are in an entirely different world. But by the end of the week, things have a way of smoothing themselves out.

Even though Penn State had a loss, this was still a game of national magnitude. The Buckeyes had passed their test at Texas, could they handle Penn State? ABC was here to find out, as was College GameDay.

Defensive tackle Quinn Pitcock stops Penn State's Tony Hunt in his tracks during the Buckeyes' Big Ten win in Columbus.

Coach Tressel leads the Buckeyes onto the field for their Big Ten showdown with Penn State. "If you want to be assured of winning the Big Ten outright, then you better win all your games," he said before the victory.

To add to the pageantry, everyone in sold out Ohio Stadium seemed to be clad in scarlet. Penn State had staged a "whiteout" in Beaver Stadium last year, but it was nothing compared to the "red sea" in the Horseshoe.

It was wet and windy at game time. The two teams punched and counter punched like a couple of heavyweight boxers throughout much of the first half, but neither could land a haymaker.

Penn State finally took a 3-0 lead on the last play of the half when Kevin Kelly converted a 21-yard field goal attempt. Kelly had missed from 23 yards on the previous play, but Malcolm Jenkins was flagged for running into the kicker and Kelly made the most of his second chance.

The statistics at halftime reflected the less than ideal weather conditions and were downright ugly. The two teams had a combined total of 183 yards in total offense – 99 by Ohio State and 84 by Penn State.

The Buckeyes had gone for the jugular early, but Troy Smith's deep pass to Ginn was intercepted at the Penn State 25, ending a streak of 152 consecutive passes without an interception for the Buckeye quarterback. That was about as exciting as it got before intermission.

The halftime program included the introduction of Ohio State's Tyson Gentry and Penn State's Adam Taliaferro. Gentry had suffered a serious spinal cord injury in the

Troy Smith gave Ohio State some breathing room with a scrambling TD pass to Brian Robiskie early in the fourth quarter that gave the Buckeyes a 14-3 lead.

Malcolm Jenkins effectively put the
game away with this interception
and 61-yard return for a touchdown.

spring and, although, still wheelchair bound was able to raise his arm and thank the fans for their encouragement and support. Taliaferro, who incurred a similar injury against Ohio State six years ago, is now almost fully recovered. The two have become friends since Gentry's injury.

Ohio State finally got on the scoreboard in the third quarter thanks to a jump start from tailback Antonio Pittman. The 5-11 junior was the catalyst on a 9-play 75-yard drive in which he had a 19-yard run and caught a 17-yard screen pass. The latter moved the ball down to the Penn State 12-yard line and Pittman bolted over right tackle on the next play to give OSU a 7-3 lead.

The Buckeyes had the lead, but they were anything but comfortable heading into the fourth quarter. That changed in the blink of an eye as Troy Smith again came to the rescue.

On second-and-nine at the Penn State 37, Smith was flushed out of the pocket and rolled to his right. Seeing no one open, he reversed his field and kept the play alive. Few people do the latter better than Smith. As Smith was improvising at midfield, Brian Robiskie broke free. Smith's pass hit Robiskie in the numbers two-yards deep in the end zone and OSU could take a deep breath at 14-3.

After the game, Kirk Barton was asked what he thought about Smith's play.

"I was thinking that when he is in New York (for the Heisman Trophy presentation), they're probably going to show that play a few times," said the big right tackle from Massillon.

Penn State didn't get to be Penn State by throwing in the towel, however. On their next possession the Nittany Lions marched down the field to the Ohio State five-yard line.

On first-and-goal Tony Hunt picked up a yard over right guard. On the next play, he followed his right tackle down to the 1-yard line. BranDon Snow got the call on third down and was stuffed by James Launinaitis and Brandon Mitchell. It was fourth-and-one. Penn State coach Joe Paterno didn't hesitate to send in a play. He was going for seven.

As the Nittany Lions prepared to run their play, the roar in Ohio Stadium was deafening. Unable to hear his quarterback, one of the Penn State linemen jumped prematurely. All of a sudden it was fourth-and-six and Paterno, who knew he could not come away empty handed, settled for a 23-yard field goal by Kelly.

On the heels of their goal-line stand, the Buckeyes recorded interceptions on Penn State's next two possessions and returned both picks for touchdowns. Just like that it was 28-6 and Penn State fans sat in disbelief.

Jenkins recorded the first pick, returning it 61 yards and atoning for running into the kicker just before halftime. Antonio Smith, who plays the corner opposite Jenkins, got the second and took his first career interception back 55 yards to the end zone.

The Buckeyes also had an earlier interception by James Laurinaitis, giving them eight on the year, three more than they had all of last year.

Penn State lost its seventh consecutive game to the Buckeyes in Ohio Stadium. In their last three home games against the Nittany Lions, all wins, the Buckeyes have scored just three offensive touchdowns, but have recorded four defensive and one special teams touchdowns. Penn State has scored a total of 38 points in its last five visits to Columbus.

The Buckeyes had now defeated both teams they had lost to in 2005. More importantly, they had started the Big Ten season on the right foot in their march toward an outright title. ◼

#24 Penn State vs #1 Ohio State (Sep 23, 2006 at Columbus, Ohio)

Score by Quarters	1	2	3	4	Score	
Penn State	0	3	0	3	6	Record: (2-2,0-1)
Ohio State	0	0	7	21	28	Record: (4-0,1-0)

Antonio Smith followed with this 55-yard interception return for another TD on the very next possession.

Something Has to Give
Ohio State 38, Iowa 17

Both Ohio State and Iowa were 4-0 on the season and 1-0 in the Big Ten. The Buckeyes were No. 1 in the Associated Press, USA Today and Harris Interactive polls, while the Hawkeyes held down the No. 13 spot in all three. So it stood to reason that something had to give when the two teams met in Iowa City.

History seemed to be on the Buckeyes' side. Ohio State led the overall series 43-14-3 and even had a 16-6-2 edge in games played in Iowa City. Still, going on the road is never easy and it can be particularly unnerving when the game is played in prime time as this one would be.

The Kinnick Stadium crowd would be in a state of frenzy by kickoff. Night games on national TV can do that, and this would be just the fifth evening soiree in Iowa history.

Additionally, in senior quarterback Drew Tate, the still relatively young Ohio State defense would face its most difficult challenge to date. A fierce competitor, Tate had almost single handedly defeated the visiting Buckeyes in 2004, engineering a very one-sided 33-7 victory. Tate would remember that game. He also would remember last year when the Buckeyes returned the favor with a 31-6 victory of their own in which he was sacked four times and the Hawkeyes were held to 137 yards of total offense in Columbus.

During the days leading up to the game, it was business as usual in the Buckeye camp.

At Tressel's Tuesday press luncheon, much of the talk centered on the visitors' pink locker room in Kinnick Stadium, designed to soothe the savage beast in Iowa's opponents.

"If you are worrying about the color of the locker room, you probably are not focusing on the task at hand," was the coach's observation.

During a radio interview with Terry Bowden and Jack Arute on Wednesday, Tressel was asked what has impressed him the most about his young defense, which already had nine takeaways on the year and had held its last three opponents to a combined total of 20 points.

"They have done a great job of keeping their poise, even though everything is brand new to them," he replied. "Much of the credit for that has to go to our two seniors up front, Quinn Pitcock and David Patterson. They have provided tremendous leadership."

Four games into the season, Pitcock and Patterson also were establishing themselves as two of the premier defensive tackles in college football, already combining for 27 tackles, 7.5 tackles-for-loss and four sacks.

"I haven't seen everyone, but it is hard to imagine a better pair of inside players than David and Quinn," stated Tressel.

The Buckeyes flew into Cedar Rapids on Friday afternoon and checked into the Clarion Hotel. Following their evening meal, they boarded the buses for the 25-minute drive to Iowa City and a brief walkthrough in the stadium.

Not only was the locker room pink in the truest Hayden Fry (former Iowa coach and the man behind the pink ploy) tradition, so was every thing in the room, including the lockers themselves and the bathroom fixtures.

But the Buckeyes, with 17 seniors on the squad had been here before. They weren't worried about the color. The

James Laurinaitis picks off a pass in front of Iowa receiver Scott Chandler during Ohio State's victory over the Hawkeyes on September 30, 2006 in Iowa City.

Quarterback Troy Smith looks out onto the field from the sidelines during Ohio State's convincing win over the Iowa Hawkeyes.

team ran threw a 40-minute rehearsal on the field and then headed back up the interstate to the hotel.

As impressive as Ohio State's win at Texas had been, there were still some doubters. If the Buckeyes could win this one, on the road, at night, and against a veteran quarterback, they were for real.

The Iowa students were calling for a "Gold Rush" and the Buckeyes were greeted by a horde of gold-shirted Hawkeye fans when they arrived at the stadium on Saturday. Chants of "Oh-ver-rated" emanated from a handful of students near the GameDay set. But the team seemed unfazed by it all.

Sometimes a game just does not live up to its hype. That would turn out to be the case on this night. In all candor, the Buckeyes were just too good for the Hawkeyes; too good on both sides of the ball.

The Buckeyes made big plays on offense and even bigger plays on defense. Add an exclamation mark to the earlier win over Texas. Tressel's team had played its best game of the year against the Hawkeyes. The final score was 38-17.

Smith was once again the catalyst on offense, completing 16 of 25 passes for 186 yards and a career-high four touchdowns. Tailback Antonio Pittman added 117 yard on the ground in a superbly balanced attack.

Two of Smith's TD passes went to wide receiver Anthony Gonzalez. The first one covered 12 yards and gave OSU a 7-0 lead on its first possession. After a 4-yard touchdown run by Pittman at the start of the second quarter, Smith connected with Roy Hall just before halftime to give the Buckeyes a 21-10 lead.

When Smith and Gonzalez hooked up on a 30-yard scoring strike on OSU's first possession of the second half, the Buckeyes had an 18-point advantage at 28-10. Smith's fourth-and-final touchdown pass came with 4:23 to play and closed out the scoring for both teams. It was a great throw by Smith in the face of pressure and maybe an even better catch by Brian Robiskie, who laid out in the back of the end zone to make the reception.

Iowa did score two touchdowns against the Buckeyes, including the first rushing touchdown of the season by an Ohio State opponent. But Tate, under pressure all game long, could never get untracked. He finished the night completing 19 of 41 passes for 249 yards, including a 4-yard touchdown throw at the start of the fourth quarter, but was intercepted three times.

Ohio State finished with 453 yards and had the ball for more than 40 minutes. Iowa finished with 253 yards and had four turnovers.

Cornerback Antonio Smith led the Buckeyes in tackles with six and safety Brandon Mitchell, whose second quarter interception led to the Buckeyes' second touchdown, had five stops and recovered a fumble. But it was a total defensive effort as the front four applied constant pressure and the linebackers made play after play after play, including fourth-quarter interceptions by James Laurinaitis and Marcus Freeman to snuff out any hope of an Iowa comeback. Defensive end Vern Gholston, one of most pleasant surprises of the season, added a pair of tackles-for-loss.

The Hawkeyes had been 0-7 when playing a No. 1 ranked team. Now they were 0-8.

The Buckeyes were 5-0 and had survived a brutal September schedule. ■

#1 Ohio State vs #13 Iowa (Sep. 30 2006 at Iowa City, IA)

Score by Quarters	1	2	3	4	Score	
Ohio State	7	14	7	10	38	Record: (5-0,2-0)
Iowa	3	7	0	7	17	Record: (4-1,1-1)

Buckeyes running back Chris Wells slips through the hands of Iowa's Miguel Merrick in the second half of OSU's romp in Iowa City.

Destiny Awaits
Ohio State 35, Bowling Green 7

In their past seven games, all victories, the Buckeyes had defeated five of the most storied programs in college football – Michigan, Notre Dame, Texas, Penn State and Iowa. Additionally, with TCU losing last week, Ohio State now owned the nation's longest winning streak at 12 consecutive victories.

All of which would mean absolutely nothing if Bowling Green left town Saturday with an upset of the top-ranked Buckeyes.

"No one walked out of Iowa City saying, 'Hey, we've arrived,'" said coach Jim Tressel at his weekly press luncheon. "I think all of our players know that as a team we can get better in every area.

"We are pleased to be 5-0. Our challenge now is to see how we handle success."

Up until the Iowa game, the Buckeyes had avoided any serious injuries. The only casualty had been senior linebacker Mike D'Andrea.

D'Andrea, from Avon Lake, Ohio, had been the most publicized linebacker in the recruiting class of 2002, even more so than classmates A. J. Hawk and Bobby Carpenter. He had size, power and could run. Boy could he run.

D'Andrea played in 13 of the Buckeyes' 14 games as a true freshman in 2002 and was ticketed for greatness. But first a shoulder injury and then a knee injury took their tolls and he wound up playing in just 17 games the next three years.

D'Andrea tried valiantly to make a comeback in 2006, but it just was not in the cards. The week of the season opener, Tressel announced that his one-time prized recruit would undergo another knee surgery that would end his college career. D'Andrea would work as a student coach in 2006 and assist Luke Fickell with Ohio State's young linebacker corps.

The Buckeyes' first in-season injury came in Iowa City. Redshirt freshman Anderson Russell, who had worked his way into the starting lineup at free safety, suffered a knee injury in the first half of the game against the Hawkeyes. A torn ACL would require surgery and he would miss the remainder of the season and the bowl game. Russell had been playing well. His loss would hurt.

With Russell out of the lineup, sophomore Jamario O'Neal received a battlefield commission. O'Neal, yet another member of the Glenville High School Alumni Club, had lettered as a true freshman, but the vast majority of his playing time had come with the special teams. Now, when the Falcons came to town, he would make his first college start.

As they had done in three of their first five games, the Buckeyes came out with guns blazing and scored on their first drive.

Troy Smith capped off an assertive nine-play, 64-yard drive with a three-yard touchdown pass to tight end Rory Nicol. It was Nicol's first touchdown reception of the year and just the second of his career.

Nicol had lettered as a true freshman in 2004, but sat out the 2005 season with a lingering foot injury. His six-pointer against the Falcons was just what the doctor ordered in terms of a confidence boost.

Bowling Green responded with an impressive opening

Antonio Pittman extended his consecutive-games touchdown streak to 11 during the Buckeyes' victory over Bowling Green, finding the end zone twice.

Freshman Kurt Coleman
(right) gets his hands on a
Bowling Green field goal
attempt in the first quarter,
leading to the drive that put
OSU up 14-0 early.

drive of its own, marching from the Falcon 18 to the Ohio State 33. But on third-and-nine, quarterback Anthony Turner misfired and coach Greg Brandon sent in the field goal unit for a 50-yard attempt.

Freshman Kurt Coleman blocked the kick and deflected it into the hands of James Laurinaitis who returned it 14 yards to the Ohio State 47. Laurinaitis, who already had four interceptions on the year, was quickly developing a reputation for being in the right place at the right time.

Nine plays later the Buckeyes had a 14-0 lead. Tailback Antonio Pittman capped off the drive with an eight-yard run around left end, extending his streak of games with a rushing touchdown to 11.

Pittman added his second touchdown of the day midway through the second quarter after defensive end Vernon Gholston intercepted a Turner pass and returned it eight yards to the BG 21-yard line. A holding penalty negated a three-yard run by Pittman and moved the ball back to the 31, but Smith hit Ted Ginn Jr. for a 10-yard gain and Roy Hall for 13 to give the Buckeyes a first-and-goal on the 8. Pittman took it from there and had his first multiple touchdown game of the year.

Smith, who began the game by completing his first eight passes, was 12-of-14 at halftime. Eight of those had gone to Ginn who was within one of his career high, set last year at Michigan.

Bowling Green got on the scoreboard in the third quarter with a 15-play, 85-yard drive. Turner hit Corey Partridge from 12 yards out for the score.

The Falcons' scoring drive ate up 8:39 on the clock. The Buckeyes first possession of the second half started with 6:21 to play in the third quarter. Smith capped off that possession 14 plays later with an 11-yard pass to split end Ray Small. The Buckeyes' drive had taken more than seven minutes and the pass to Small came with 14:03 remaining in the game.

Earlier in the week Small had told Smith he would score against Bowling Green if Smith would get him the ball. After the game, Tressel laughingly called his budding young star "a soothsayer."

Smith then completed his day's work with a 57-yard scoring strike to Ginn. Smith had three touchdown passes on the day and seven in his last two games. Ginn had a career-high 10 receptions for 122 yards.

The 57-yard completion marked the eighth play of 50 or more yards from Smith to Ginn over the past two and a half seasons.

The Buckeyes finished with 387 yards compared to 339 for the Falcons, who actually out-rushed OSU. Laurinaitis and cornerback Malcom Jenkins each had nine tackles to pace the Buckeyes, who for the fourth time in six games had held their opponent to seven points or less.

"It wasn't our best effort, but the bottom line is it was a win and we can learn from it," said Tressel. "From now on it is all Big Ten. Everyone in the league either has a loss or has to come through us. We control our own destiny." ■

Bowling Green vs #1 Ohio State (Oct 7, 2006 at Columbus, Ohio)

Score by Quarters	1	2	3	4	Score	
Bowling Green	0	0	7	0	7	Record: (3-3)
Ohio State	14	7	0	14	35	Record: (6-0)

Troy Smith completed 17 of 20 passes for 190 yards and three TDs, with 10 of those completions and a 57-yard touchdown going to fellow Heisman Trophy candidate Ted Ginn Jr.

Beware of the Spartan Hex
Ohio State 38, Michigan State 7

Michigan State had driven a stake into the heart of Ohio State's national championship hopes on more than one occasion. Most recently, the 1998 Spartans pulled the rug out from under the top-ranked Buckeyes with a stunning 28-24 victory in Ohio Stadium. The Spartans, who were 4-4 coming into the game, rallied from a 24-9 deficit midway through the third quarter. Ohio State would go on to post an 11-1 record and finish third in the final polls, but the sting of that loss is still felt today by the likes of Joe Germaine, David Boston, Michael Wiley, Ahmed Plummer, Andy Katzenmoyer and Antoine Winfield just to name a few. Their chance at immortality was gone as quickly as you can say "Go Green."

In 1974, the Buckeyes were ranked No. 1 and had rolled over their first eight opponents by an average of 36 points a game. Levi Jackson's 88-yard run (probably the most famous play in MSU football history) gave the Spartans a 16-13 lead with 3:17 remaining. Back came the Buckeyes, marching down the field as the clock ticked off precious seconds. On first down at the MSU 11-yard line, All-America tailback Archie Griffin picked up 5. On the next play, Cornelius Greene handed the ball to fullback Champ Henson who bulled his way down close to the goal line. It appeared from the press box that Henson had gotten in, but the officials spotted the ball just short of the stripe. The clock was running as the Buckeyes attempted to huddle and run one final play. On the center snap, the ball bounced away from Greene, but was picked up by wingback Brian Baschnagel who darted into the end zone for what would have been the winning score. As one official signaled touchdown, two others indicated time had expired. With that, the officials ran to the locker room and even though it took 46 minutes to receive an official ruling from Big Ten Commissioner Wayne Duke, the game was over.

In 1972, Michigan State fans celebrated by tearing down the goal posts after the Spartans upended the Buckeyes, 19-12, in East Lansing. The decidedly underdog Spartans had dedicated the game to veteran Coach Duffy Daugherty who earlier in the week had announced his retirement. The loss ended the Buckeyes' seven-game winning streak and knocked them from the unbeaten ranks. Griffin fumbled twice in the game, which didn't set particularly well with Buckeye coach Woody Hayes. As a matter of fact, the following week at Northwestern, Henson would set a school record with 44 carries, while Archie had just two. Woody had a way of making his point. The loss to the 4-4 Spartans was the only loss of the regular season for the Buckeyes who would go on to share the Big Ten title and play in the first of four consecutive Rose Bowls.

Those three examples should indicate why no one on the 2006 Buckeye team was taking Michigan State for granted. Even though the 3-3 Spartans had lost three in a row, they had talented players and a win over Ohio State would make their season.

The leader of the Michigan State attack was quarterback Drew Stanton. He and Buckeye signal caller Troy Smith had gotten to know one another over the summer at an EA Sports

AP/Wide World

OSU running back Antonio Pittman runs into Michigan State defender Greg Cooper during the first quarter of their Big Ten showdown in East Lansing on October 14, 2006.

Ohio State stars Brian Robiskie (80), Troy Smith (10) and Ted Ginn Jr. (7) celebrate a score against the Spartans during the Buckeyes' Big Ten win in East Lansing.

Camp and had continued their friendship into the season.

Asked to compare the two, Ohio State coach Jim Tressel said, "They are both competitors and they are both tough and you know how I feel about toughness in a quarterback. It is the most important thing."

Still the Spartans were 3-3 and in a tailspin. To make matters worse, in their Notre Dame game, they had lost running back Javon Ringer with a season-ending knee injury. Ringer was one of the top backs in the Big Ten and his loss was significant.

"Given the way Michigan State has played the last three games, what do you say to your team about them?" queried ABC analyst Bob Griese in a teleconference call to Tressel.

"Fortunately, we have played them the past three years and the players on this team know Michigan State could have won all three of those games," was the coach's reply. "We tell them it is Michigan State."

Prior to that teleconference call with the ABC announce crew of Griese, Brad Nessler, Paul Maguire and Bonnie Bernstein, Tressel received some uplifting news. Bob Gentry, Tyson's father, had emailed assistant coach Darrell Hazel to let him know Tyson had moved his toes. Hazel was all smiles as he stuck his head around the corner to let Tressel know. This game was important, many people saw it as the last real test before the season finale against

Chance Brockway Jr.

Curtis Terry (55) slams the brakes on a MSU ballcarrier during Ohio State's victory on October 14, 2006.

Michigan on Nov. 18, but for the time being all of Tressel's thoughts were focused on one of his players. That is the kind of guy Jim Tressel is.

Two tornadoes actually touched down in Columbus on Wednesday and while the storms had passed by Thursday, it was cold and very windy, making practice conditions less than ideal.

After Thursday's practice as Tressel was preparing to meet with the media, he said to Hazel, "I have never seen anyone who can throw the ball in the wind the way Troy can. His passes just don't change. It's amazing."

Upon arrival in East Lansing, the team went immediately to Spartan Stadium. As Tressel took a few minutes to go over some last minute details in the locker room, he had the absolute undivided attention of every player.

This team was focused. There would be no upset if these players had their way.

Early in the week, the forecast for Saturday had been for possible showers. Instead it turned out to be a beautiful, although, slightly on the chilly side fall afternoon with no sign of precipitation.

Michigan State won the coin toss and deferred, electing to kick. Given the Buckeyes' explosive offense that choice might seem somewhat baffling, but when freshman tailback Chris "Beanie" Wells fumbled on OSU's third play from scrimmage, the Spartans had the ball at the Ohio State 31 yards line.

Spartan fans sensed an upset as Ohio State fans muttered "Not again."

But as the Ohio State players had said so many times during the week. This was not the same team that lost in 1998.

On MSU's first play from scrimmage Stanton hit running back Jehuu Caulcrick who wove his way down to the OSU 14. But the Spartans were called for holding and the ball came back to the 24. On first-and-three, Caulcrick was dropped for a loss by defensive end Jay Richardson. On the next play, Stanton's pass to Terry Love was incomplete.

Now it was third-and-five. Stanton again dropped back, but before he could get rid of the ball, linebacker James Laurinaitis was in his face. Stanton retreated in an attempt to get away, but Laurinaitis sacked him for a 16-yard loss, taking the Spartans out of field goal range.

The young Ohio State defense had come through again.

Ohio State took over at its own 20 following the Michigan State punt. Smith expertly moved his team down the field, hitting three of four passes, including a 37-yard strike to flanker Ted Ginn Jr. Tailback Antonio Pittman capped off the 12-play drive with a two yard run behind center Doug Datish and right guard T. J. Downing and the Buckeyes had a 7-0 lead and would never look back.

Pittman's touchdown was his eight of the year, surpassing his total of seven the previous season, and gave him at least one rushing touchdown in 12 consecutive games. He and Northern Illinois running back had shared the longest streak in the nation, but Wolfe's string came to an end earlier that day against Western Michigan.

It was early, but the Spartans were reeling.

At the beginning of the second quarter, Michigan State went for it on fourth-and-2 at the Ohio State 36-yard line. Stanton's sneak gained only a yard, however, and the Buckeyes took over at their own 35. Two runs by Chris Wells and a 32-yard completion to Anthony Gonzalez moved the ball to the MSU 19. But the MSU stiffened and the Buckeyes had to settle for a 32-yard field goal by Aaron Pettrey. It was the start of a 17-point quarter for the Buckeyes, who after punting the ball away on their next possession, forced the Spartans to punt from deep in their own end zone.

Michigan State coach John L. Smith could either punt it out of bounds or risk punting to Buckeye comet Ted Ginn Jr., which is a little bit like choosing your own poison. He chose to kick to Ginn and the result was lethal. Gathering the ball in at his own forty and getting a block from Anthony Gonzalez, Ginn split a pair of MSU defenders and

AP/Wide World

Nick Patterson (23) and Kurt Coleman (4) try in vain to prevent MSU's A.J. Jimmerson from scoring the Spartans' lone TD of the day in the fourth quarter of the Buckeyes' 38-7 victory in East Lansing.

then raced 60 yards to the end zone. It was his sixth career punt return for a touchdown, giving him sole possession of the Big Ten record that he had shared with Iowa's Tim Dwight. It also left him two shy of the NCAA record.

Buckeye fans had been waiting all year for Ginn to break one. The 10-000 or so Ohio State fans who had made the trek from Columbus to East Lansing that day got their wish.

On Michigan State's next possession, Stanton dropped back to pass on first-and-ten at his own 48, but OSU linebacker Marcus Freeman jumped in front of the intended receiver and picked off his second interception of the year, giving the Buckeyes possession on the MSU 39. It was the Buckeyes' 13th interception of the year and gave them one in each of the first eight games.

After a holding penalty on OSU, Smith and Gonzalez hooked up on a 23-yard completion taking the ball down to the MSU 26. A nine-yard pass to Ginn and a five-yard run by Smith made it first-and-10 on the 12. But after two straight incompletions, the Buckeyes called time out with 47 seconds remaining.

On the ensuing play Smith was forced to scramble, but somehow found Gonzalez on a crossing route in the back of the end zone. A perfect pass to his outstretched hands, and the ensuing extra point, made it 24-0. Game over!

"Troy put it the only place he could put it it if I was going to catch it. It was an amazing throw," said Gonzalez.

Ohio State kicked off to start the second half. The Spartans picked up a first down on their first play from scrimmage on a 10-yard run by Caulcrick. But Stanton was sacked on a third-and-nine by the Buckeyes' Quinn Pitcock and the Spartans were again forced to punt.

As Gonzalez signaled for a fair catch, an MSU player ran into him and was flagged for interference. The Buckeyes took over at their own 47 and five plays later had a 31-0 lead on a seven-yard pass from Smith to Robiskie. On the play, Smith spun out of one tackle and then broke another before firing a dart to the diving Robiskie. It was a play that almost certainly would appear on SportsCenter later that night.

Ohio State scored again in the fourth period to up the count to 38-0. Michigan State got on the board with just over a minute to play to avoid the shutout.

The Buckeyes rolled up 421 yards against the Spartans, throwing for 239 yards and rushing for 182 more. Smith hit 15 of 22 passes for 234 yards and a pair of touchdowns and also rushed for 19 yards. Gonzalez led all receivers with seven receptions for 118 yards and a score. The seven receptions gave him 34 on the year, six more than he had all of last year.

The OSU defense, meanwhile, limited the Spartans to 198 total yards, including just 63 on the ground. Laurinaitis led the Buckeyes with nine tackles, the sixth time in seven games that he has paced the team, and Pitcock added two more sacks to his resume, giving him a team-leading seven on the year.

The last minute, or nearly so, touchdown by the Spartans lowered the Buckeyes average points allowed to 9.0 points a game, but knocked them out of the national lead.

No matter, the Buckeyes had avoided the upset, in the process becoming just the 20th team in Ohio State history to jump out to a 7-0 start. ■

#1 Ohio State vs Michigan State (Oct 14, 2006 at East Lansing, Mich.)

Score by Quarters	1	2	3	4	Score	
Ohio State	7	17	7	7	38	Record: (7-0,3-0)
Michigan State	0	0	0	7	7	Record: (3-4,0-3)

Chance Brockway Jr.

Joel Penton puts the clamps on Michigan State quarterback Drew Stanton during OSU's victory over the Spartans.

Hurryin' Past the Hoosiers
Ohio State 44, Indiana 3

Once the Buckeyes got by Michigan State, they were supposed to have clear sailing until the season finale against Michigan. Ohio State's next three opponents – Indiana, Illinois and Northwestern, in that order – had a combined record of 8 wins and 13 losses. Only the Wolverines on Nov. 18 stood in the way of the Buckeyes' second trip in five years to the national championship game.

Indiana had the best credentials of the three pre-Michigan opponents. Coach Terry Hoeppenrs' Hoosiers were 4-3 on the year and 2-1 in the Big Ten. They were coming to town with a two-game winning streak after downing Illinois on the road and recording a stunning upset of 13th-ranked Iowa in Bloomington. They had overcome double-digit deficits in three of their four wins and the victories over Illinois and Iowa represented their first back-to-back Big Ten wins since 2001.

The Hoosiers played with the indomitable spirit of their head coach. Hoeppner, who is in his third year at Indiana after a very successful career at Miami (O.), is both a motivator and a fierce competitor. He demands, and gets, the most out of his players, in the process convincing them that no mountain is too high to climb.

He is also an example of courage. Diagnosed with a brain tumor in the spring, he has since undergone two operations, one of which came after the season started. He also endured the loss of his closest friend Northwestern head coach Randy Walker, who died unexpectedly of a heart attack in July.

"Indiana is a lot like their coach," said Tressel. "They are tough and courageous. You don't come back from big deficits the way they have unless you have a lot of character. It is fun to watch them on film, because they play with such effort. They are a team on the rise."

They had certainly been so the past two weeks. The win over once-beaten Iowa, whose only previous loss had been to Ohio State, was particularly impressive. It was no fluke; the Hoosiers had outplayed the Hawkeyes.

But as the Buckeyes prepared for the Hoosiers' visit to Columbus, the game itself took a back seat to the Big Ten announcement that ESPNU would televise the game.

Only one of the three cable systems in Columbus had ESPNU and the only other way to get the game was on DirecTV. For most, there would be no live television coverage. Fans were enraged and the cacophony was deafening.

E-mails and phone calls flooded the Athletics Department. Most of the latter were short and to the point and would not meet the criteria needed for a "PG" rating.

Ohio State Director of Athletics Gene Smith tried, albeit unsuccessfully, to convince ESPN to allow one of the local over-the-air stations to air the game. When his pleas fell on deaf ears, Smith engineered an agreement with Tom Griesdorn of WBNS-TV and Chuck Gerber of ESPN that would allow the game to be shown on a delayed basis on both Saturday and Sunday nights. It wasn't live, but it was the next best thing.

The other option was to listen to the game on the radio. Paul Keels and Jim Lachey, who do the play-by-play and color for WBNS Radio, are two of the best around and

OSU quarterback Troy Smith takes to the ground on this play, but he put up monster passing numbers once again against Indiana, throwing for four more TDs-all in the first half.

many fans routinely turn down the volume on their TV sets to listen to them. But it is one thing to have the option to do so and another to have no choice. ESPNU was not an acceptable option to Ohio State fans.

The first Bowl Championship Series rankings of the year were released Sunday. Ohio State was a solid No. 1, becoming the first Big Ten team to sit atop the initial BCS standings. Southern Cal was second and Michigan third.

"We appreciate the recognition of our difficult schedule, but we realize the only poll that counts is the final one," said Tressel.

Two other major announcements came during the week: Senior defensive tackle Quinn Pitcock had been named as a semi-finalist for the Lombardi Award and sophomore linebacker James Laurinaitis was a semi-finalist for the Butkus Award. Both lists would be pared down in late November. Right now, the task at hand was beating the Hoosiers and becoming the 14th team in Ohio State history to start the season with an 8-0 record.

It was a noon kickoff and the crowd for some reason was slow to arrive. Indiana took an early 3-0 lead on a 34-yard field goal by Austin Starr. Tracy Porter's 34-yard punt return had given the Hoosiers prime field position at the Ohio State 15-yard line. But thanks to a couple of dropped passes, IU had to settle for three. Still, they had the lead and it was only the third time all year that the Buckeyes had trailed.

Ohio State punted on its first two possessions as Troy Smith uncharacteristically misfired on his first three pass attempts. Fortunately, that was not to be a harbinger of things to come.

On the Buckeyes' next possession, Smith was again off target on his first pass. On second-and-ten, though, he found tailback Antonio Pittman alone in the flat on a screen pass. Pittman picked up 22 yards and just that quickly the Buckeyes were untracked.

Smith kept things going with a 29-yard run on which he started to roll to his right and then reversed his field and raced down the near sideline in front of the Ohio State bench to the Indiana 32. Two plays later, on third-and-one, Smith faked an inside handoff to his running back and calmly lofted the ball into the hands of tight end Rory Nicol, who waltzed untouched into the end zone.

Smith seemingly provides a Heisman Trophy type of play each game. He did so against the Hoosiers on the Buckeyes' next possession.

The Buckeyes had taken over at their own 47 and in three plays had moved to the Indiana 31. On first down, Smith dropped back to pass, was pressured, pirouetted out of danger and rolled to his left. There was an open field in front of him. But instead of running the ball, he suddenly pulled up, took a step back and let the ball go. Somehow, he had seen Ted Ginn Jr. running to daylight. Ginn and the ball became one in the corner of the end zone and Ohio State led 14-3. Smith had provided another Heisman moment.

The Buckeyes' lead ballooned to 21-3 on their next possession as Smith threw his third touchdown of the day, this time a five-yard strike to Anthony Gonzalez. Gonzalez also had a 24-yard reception earlier in the drive

Given Indiana's history of successful comebacks this year, the Buckeyes were not about to sit on their lead when they got the ball back with 51 seconds remaining in the half.

Taking over at the Indiana 49, Smith and split end Brian Robiskie hooked up on consecutive completions and, with the aid of a personal foul, the Buckeyes had a first-and-goal at the 1-yard line. Smith then threw a perfect pass to tight end Jake Ballard who was running a drag route five-yards in the end zone and Ohio State had a 28-3 lead at the half.

The three-play drive had taken all of 31 seconds. It was the first reception of the year for Ballard, a highly regarded true freshman from Springboro, Ohio.

"When a senior quarterback throws the ball to a freshman who hasn't played very much, you better catch it," said Ballard after the game.

At halftime, OSU had 272 yards in total offense, while

Ted Ginn Jr. goes airborne to haul in a 31-yard TD pass from Troy Smith.

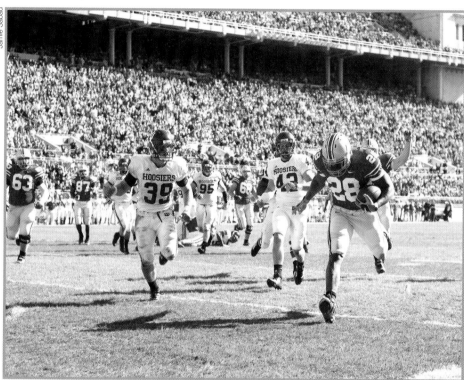

Running back Chris Wells finishes up the scoring with a 12-yard scamper against Indiana.

"We practice and practice and practice that play and watch duck after duck after duck," joked Smith after the game. "But Ted kept telling us if he got the chance in a game he would throw a spiral, and he did."

With the OSU defense on its way to a season-high 44 points, the Buckeyes' defense

While the OSU offense was on its way to a season-high 44 points, the Buckeye defense in general, and cornerback Antonio Smith in particular, were keeping plenty of heat on the Hoosiers. Smith was Lewis' worst nightmare, finishing the game with a career-high 12 tackles, including four tackles-for-loss and a sack and a forced fumble. Eleven of his tackles were solos.

Indiana had just 65. Hoosier quarterback Kellen Lewis is going to be a good one, but on this day at least, he was no match for the Buckeyes, whose variety of stunts and blitz packages never allowed him to get into any kind of rhythm.

Halloween was still two weeks away, but the Buckeyes reached into their bag of tricks in the second half as Ginn took the pitch from Smith on apparent reverse and then delivered a perfect spiral to Nicol whose defender had been tripped up by the turf monster. Nicol gathered in the ball and scored his second touchdown of the day and the third by a tight end. The play covered 32 yards.

After the game as the team was heading to the locker room, a zealous fan urged the OSU coaching staff to start a Heisman campaign for Antonio Smith.

"Every time I looked up he was making a play," conceded Tressel.

On Monday, both Smiths were honored by the Big Ten – Troy, who threw for 220 yards and tied a personal high with his four touchdown passes, as the co-offensive player of the week and Antonio, the former walk-on, as the co-defensive player of the week.

The Buckeyes were 8-0 and 4-0 at the halfway point of the Big Ten season. ■

Indiana vs #1 Ohio State (Oct 21, 2006 at Columbus, Ohio)

Score by Quarters	1	2	3	4	Score	
Indiana	3	0	0	0	3	Record: (4-4,2-2)
Ohio State	7	21	10	6	44	Record: (8-0,4-0)

Tight end Rory Nicol catches one of two touchdown passes in the Buckeyes' rout of Indiana-one from Troy Smith and another from Ted Ginn.

Striking Gold
Ohio State 44, Minnesota 0

One of the battle cries of the team during pre-season camp was "Get Through September." The Buckeyes had done so with a 5-0 record, solidifying their No. 1 ranking with impressive road wins over Texas and Iowa.

Jim Tressel's team had extended that record to 8-0 with three more wins in the month of October and had a solid lead in each of the first two Bowl Championship series rankings.

To get to 9-0, all the Buckeyes had to do was defeat Minnesota. On paper, anyway, that did not appear to be a problem. The Gophers, riddled by injuries, were 3-5 on the year and 0-4 in the Big Ten.

Still, Minnesota was coached by Glen Mason and that in itself was cause for concern. "Mace" had played for the Buckeyes, under Woody Hayes, and later returned as an assistant coach at his alma mater between 1978 and 1985. When he left Ohio State to become the head coach at Kent State, he was the Buckeyes' offensive coordinator and regarded as one of the up-and-coming young coaches in college football. From Kent, Mason had gone on to Kansas before settling in at Minnesota at the start of the 1997 season.

Mason has always had a soft spot in his heart for Ohio State and was very much in the running to replace John Cooper in 2001 when Tressel got the nod. He would have his team ready to play when it came to Columbus. This was Homecoming weekend on the OSU campus and one of its alums was coming home.

Additionally, the Minnesota roster was dotted with players from the Central Ohio area, all eager to show their families and friends that the Buckeyes had made a mistake not recruiting them. They wanted their visit to Ohio Stadium to be a memorable one.

And there was one other factor to consider. Tressel's record at Ohio State was a glittering 58-13, including a 34-10 record in Big Ten play, but seven of his 13 losses had come in October and this was Halloween weekend.

As had seemed to be the pattern this fall it rained throughout the week. On Thursday and Friday more than an inch-and-a-half of rain fell on the central Ohio area. For the most part the rain had stopped by Saturday morning, but it was the first cold day of the year with temperatures hovering in the mid 40s, and by the 3:30 p.m. kickoff the winds were gusting up to 35 miles an hour. Not the kind of weather conditions conducive to Ohio State's stellar passing attack.

Minnesota won the toss and deferred, like most teams preferring to take the ball in the second half.

Ted Ginn Jr. was deep for the Buckeyes. Ginn had broken his toe while hurrying to a wide receivers meeting the Wednesday before the Indiana game. He had played against the Hoosiers with no ill effects before news of the injury became public. He also practiced on Thursday before the IU game. But once the news got out, everyone was anxious to see if it would be the same old Ted Ginn out there.

The question was answered in a hurry. Ginn took the opening kickoff at his own 8 and returned it 35 yards to the Ohio State 43 yard line. Apparently, it took more than a broken toe to slow down the Ginn express.

Jamie Sabau

Antonio Pittman, who'd seen his touchdown streak of 12 straight games end a week before the Minnesota game, scored twice for good measure.

Chapter 12

The Buckeyes quickly took advantage of their favorable field position, marching 57 yards in eight plays for a 7-0 lead.

Tailback Antonio Pittman, who a week earlier had seen his string of 12 straight games with at least one rushing touchdown ended, carried the ball five times on the drive, including the final 10 yards for the score.

The Buckeyes also scored on their next possession as Aaron Pettrey hooked the ball through the uprights for 42 yards away, despite the whirling winds.

It was 10-0 after two possessions and the Buckeyes didn't seem to be spooked in the slightest.

Then, just for a minute, the Gophers put a hex on the Buckeyes, who fumbled on their next two possessions.

First, freshman tailback Beanie Wells put the ball on the ground at the Minnesota 9. Then, after the OSU defense had forced a punt and the Buckeyes had the ball back, quarterback Troy Smith had the ball stripped as he was trying to avoid a sack. Minnesota recovered at the Ohio State 38. Again the defense held, this time stopping Amir Pinnix on fourth-and-one at the OSU 29. The officials didn't even bother to measure.

The offense, somewhat red faced, high-fived the defense as it came off the field and then went to work with a renewed sense of purpose.

With Smith in total command, the Buckeyes moved downfield to the Minnesota 18. On second-and-eight Smith checked off to Brian Robiskie who ran a simple go-route and caught his fourth touchdown pass of the season in the corner of the end zone. It was a perfectly thrown pass. If the strong-armed Smith was affected by the wind, he certainly didn't show it.

The Buckeyes were ahead 17-0 at halftime.

The halftime activities featured the introduction of the 1961 team on hand for its 45th reunion. That team had posted an 8-0-1 record and had captured the Big Ten title with a 6-0 mark. The returning players, all a little grayer now, received a warm welcome from the Homecoming crowd of 105,443. But the biggest ovation came moments later when the OSU Marching Band performed their famous Script Ohio and OSU alumnus Jack Nicklaus made his way out on to the field as the honorary "I" dotter.

Nicklaus, the former OSU All-American and NCAA champion and the winner of 18 major titles on the PGA tour, became just the fifth non-band member to dot the "I". Bob Hope and Woody Hayes were two of the others in a very exclusive fraternity.

Nicklaus, who had most of his family with him, was obviously honored and made it a point to acknowledge the crowd by waving his ball cap, which, was the same style that Woody Hayes had worn as coach of the Buckeyes.

Nicklaus had grown up in Upper Arlington, Ohio and had entertained the idea of playing football. But Woody quickly set him straight on that point, all but ordering him to stick to golf. As it turned out, that was pretty good advice.

Ohio State kicked off to start the second half. Minnesota took over at its own 20, but on third-and-10, Antonio Smith picked off Brian Cupito's pass and returned it 8 yards to the Gopher 23. Three plays later, Troy Smith scored his first rushing touchdown of the season on a 21-yard run on which his juke left a defender frozen in his tracks at about the 12-yard line. It was one of those highlight plays that would make SportsCenter later that night.

"That play just won him the Heisman," declared former OSU coach turned radio analyst Earle Bruce,

Regardless the Buckeyes, whose scoring drive took all of 71 seconds, were ahead 24-0.

Pittman made it 30-0 on a 13 yard run on Ohio State's next possession. The Buckeyes had taken over at the Minnesota 41 after an athletic interception by safety Jamario O'Neal. It was O'Neal's first career interception, but the third of the afternoon by the Buckeyes, raising their season total to 18. The PAT attempt was blocked, but the outcome of the game had long since been decided.

Ohio State added a pair of rushing touchdowns in the

Troy Smith breaks free for some running yardage in OSU's victory over the Golden Gophers.

Brian Robiskie hauls in an 18-yard pass from Troy Smith in the second quarter of the Buckeyes' rout of Minnesota.

fourth quarter, giving them five rushing TDs on the day. Beanie Wells scored the first on a 3-yard run and Quarterback Justin Zwick the second on a 1-yard sneak. It was the first career rushing touchdown for Zwick, who is a fifth-year senior.

The Buckeye defense, meanwhile, was making life miserable for the Gophers, holding them to 182 yards of total offense, including just 47 yards rushing on 26 attempts. When the clock hit 0:00, the Buckeyes had their first shutout since a 20-0 blanking of Northwestern in 2003.

Additionally, the defense extended its string of consecutive quarters without allowing a touchdown to eight. In the last four games, OSU had surrendered just 17 points. On the year, seven of their nine opponents had been held to seven points or less.

Ohio State had gotten through the month of October unscathed. Halloween was not so kind to some of the other ranked teams that day. ■

Minnesota vs #1 Ohio State (Oct 28, 2006 at Columbus, Ohio)

Score by Quarters	1	2	3	4	Score	
Minnesota	0	0	0	0	0	Record: (3-6,0-5)
Ohio State	10	7	13	14	44	Record: (9-0,5-0)

Joel Penton (98) and James Laurinaitis (33) helped anchor an OSU defense that recorded its first shutout since 2003 and that had allowed only 17 points in its last four games.

Too Close for Comfort
Ohio State 17, Illinois 10

Through the first nine games of the year, Ohio State was steamrolling over its opposition by an average of 28 points a game. In their last two games, the Buckeyes had outscored Indiana and Minnesota by a combined total of 88-3.

Come to think of it, no one had really given Jim Tressel's team much of a tussle in either September or October. The 24-7 victory at Texas in week two of the season had been the closest game. Penn State had kept it interesting for a while and, to be fair, so had Iowa, but in both cases the Buckeyes pulled away in the third quarter and put the hammer down in the fourth.

But this was the first week in November, and as former Buckeye coach Earle Bruce used to warn, "It's the pretenders in September and the contenders in November."

The first November hurdle for the Buckeyes would be Illinois. The Illini are coached by Ron Zook, a native of Loudonville, Ohio, a Miami of Ohio graduate and a former Ohio State assistant coach under John Cooper between 1988 and 1990.

Zook is now in his second year with the Illini after three years as the head coach at the University of Florida. His first Illinois team finished with a 2-9 record and this year's squad was 2-7 and had won just one of five Big Ten games. Still, the Illini had defeated Michigan State in East Lansing, and they were coming off an ever-so-close 30-24 loss at Wisconsin. Led by quarterback Juice Williams, a true freshman, they had built a commanding lead against the Badgers, but couldn't hold on down the stretch – a common problem for young teams.

Williams was an undeniable talent. Ohio State had recruited him hard. Many observers compared him favorably to the Buckeyes' own signal caller Troy Smith. But Williams, who prepped at Chicago Vocational High School, had elected to stay home and play for Zook.

During his three years at Ohio State, Zook had developed a reputation as a tireless recruiter. Players loved his infectious enthusiasm. He has been able to recruit players wherever he has been and Illinois was proving to be no exception. Landing Juice Williams proved that.

"Illinois is an improving team," warned Tressel. "They play hard and they don't quit. We can't go over there thinking this will be easy, because it won't."

The Buckeye coach was speaking from experience. In 1983, Ohio State dropped a 17-13 decision in Champaign. Two years later, OSU lost again to the host Illini, dropping a 31-28 verdict when Coach Mike White's son, Chris, kicked the winning field goal as time ran out. Tressel was an assistant coach for the Buckeyes on both occasions. In 2002, Tressel's second year as the head coach at Ohio State, the Buckeyes escaped with a 23-16 overtime win in Memorial Stadium en route to a perfect 14-0 record and the national championship.

Such cautious rhetoric appears to be just so much "coach speak" to most fans. They would learn differently on Saturday, however. The Buckeyes would be in a dogfight.

The game, the 93rd meeting between the two teams, started out the way most of the first nine games had begun.

Ohio State wideout Anthony Gonzalez fights his way to extra yardage after a catch against Illinois in Champaign on November 4, 2006.

OSU players show solidarity during the Illinois game in Champaign on November 4, 2006.

Illinois won the toss and deferred. Ohio State immediately took the ball and marched down field for a touchdown.

Chris Wells got the Buckeyes on the board with a 2-yard run with 8:16 to play in the first quarter, capping off a 14-play, 80-yard drive for the Buckeyes. Troy Smith hit four-of-five passes on the drive and picked up 10 yards on a third-and-nine from the Illinois 10-yard line, paving the way for the TD by Wells.

The Buckeyes made it 14-0 early in the second quarter on a 1-yard run by Antonio Pittman. The drive started on the short side of the 50 after the Buckeyes' Curtis Terry recovered an Illinois fumble at the Illini 38. Defensive end Lawrence Wilson, who had been coming on in practice of late and had earned more playing time, forced the fumble.

When Ohio State added a 50-yard field goal by Aaron Pettrey just before half, it looked like business as usual as the two teams exited the field.

But in the Illinois locker room, where Red Grange and Dick Butkus had become legends, Ron Zook wasn't about to throw in the towel. With 30 minutes to play, he believed his team was still in it. On the other side of the field, Tressel knew the same thing.

Ohio State had 195 yards of total offense in the first half, compared to just 72 for Illinois. And while the Buckeyes struggled to move the ball against a variety of Illinois stunts in the third quarter, neither team scored and Ohio State seemed to be in control in every way.

Buckeye Ted Ginn Jr. averts Illinois tackler Jody Ellis during OSU's 17-10 win at Illinois.

Ted Ginn gains extra yardage after getting tripped up by Illinois' Brit Miller during the Buckeyes' Big Ten conquest on November 4, 2006.

After all, the Buckeye defense had extended its string of scoreless quarters to 10 and had not allowed a touchdown in the last 11 quarters. Members of the fourth estate in the press box were hurriedly checking their media guides in an effort to find the last time the Buckeyes had recorded back-to-back shutouts. As it turned out, they wouldn't need that statistic.

With 11:23 to play in the game, Illinois took over at the Ohio State 47-yard line after a 37-yard punt by A. J. Trapasso. Trapasso, another in a long line of outstanding punters that Tressel has pulled out of his hat at Ohio State, had let one slip off the side of his foot, very uncharacteristic

of the usually dependable sophomore.

Aided by a short field, the Illini moved to the Ohio State 26 in two plays and then were the beneficiary of a pass interference call against the Buckeyes that gave them a first down on the Ohio State 11. Sometimes the guys in the striped shirts get it wrong; they're only human. But they were dead on the money with this call. Cornerback Malcolm Jenkins and safety Brandon Mitchell had run over the intended receiver like a runaway Mack Truck. But by doing so they had saved a sure touchdown.

After picking up just one yard on the next three plays, the Illini were forced to settle for a field goal. Jason Reda's 27-yard kick was good and Illinois had avoided the shutout.

Buckeye fans were miffed, but not particularly worried. That soon changed, however.

AP/Wide World

Troy Smith is downed by Illinois' Jeremy Leman after a short running gain in the Buckeyes' 17-10 win in Champaign.

On the Buckeyes' next possession, Troy Smith was intercepted for the first time in 144 attempts and the orange-clad Illinois student section came to life in anticipation.

But momentum can be a funny thing and when OSU linebacker James Laurinaitis picked off a Tim Brasic pass on the very next play, the ecstasy subsided.

But the Buckeyes could not capitalize on the Laurinatis interception and had to punt, giving Illinois the ball at its own 20 with 3:43 to play.

After Brasic missed his first two passes, Zook, who had yanked Williams in the third quarter, re-inserted his star freshman.

"We couldn't get Juice calmed down out there, so we had decided to sit him a while," said Zook at his postgame press conference. "But with the game on the line, I wanted him in there."

Williams responded by hitting three straight passes, the first for 24 yards, the second – a flea-flicker – for 15 and the third for 10 more. All of a sudden, the Illini were at the Ohio State 35.

But on his next pass attempt, Williams was leveled by linebacker James Laurinaitis who came through untouched and was at full speed when he squeezed the last drop of juice out of the Illinois quarterback.

Back came Brasic whose three consecutive completions moved the ball down to the OSU 3-yard line. On the next play, Rashard Mendenhall took the handoff, veered to his right and powered his way into the end zone, somehow escaping the clutches of defensive end Jay Richardson. The Buckeyes' lead was down to seven.

It was the first touchdown the Buckeyes had given up in three weeks and it was just the second rushing TD of the year by an Ohio State opponent.

It was a seven-point game and everyone knew the onside kick was coming. The ball seemed to bounce either by or through three or four players before the Buckeyes' Brian Robiskie covered it at the Illinois 47-yard line with 1:40 to play. Robiskie immediately jumped up and handed the ball to the official and then accepted the congratulations of his teammates before heading back out on to the field for what he hoped would be the Buckeyes' final possession.

The Illini still had two timeouts remaining so the game was far from over. After three Antonio Pittman rushes into the teeth of the Illinois defense used up all but 18 seconds of the clock, Trapasso got a chance to redeem himself. He responded with a 55-yard punt that Austin Spitler downed on the Illinois 2-yard line with four seconds remaining in the game.

It would take a miracle now. In desperation, Zook tried a gadget play, but the Illinois receiver stepped out of bounds at his own 8 and the game was over.

Ohio State had been tested for the first time this year and had passed the test. Good teams find a way to win close games.

"Illinois played us hard and never quit," said Smith, whose Buckeyes were actually out-gained by the Illini. "My hat is off to them; they gave us all we wanted."

The 2006 Buckeyes had become just the fifth Ohio State team to win 10 games in a season. But getting fatheaded wasn't an option. Northwestern was up next and earlier in the day the Wildcats had upset Iowa, 21-7, in Iowa City. ∎

Illinois vs #1 Ohio State (Nov 4, 2006 at Champagne, IL)

Score by Quarters	1	2	3	4	Score	
Ohio State	7	10	0	0	17	OSU (10-0, 6-0)
Illinois	0	0	0	10	10	Ill. (2-7, 1-5)

Ohio State coach Jim Tressel (right) shakes hands with Illinois coach Ron Zook after the Buckeyes escaped with a hard-fought 17-10 win over the Illini in Champaign-their toughest test of the season to that point.

First Class, All the Way
Ohio State 54, Northwestern 10

It was late Sunday afternoon, almost dinner time. Anthony Gonzalez and Jim Tressel were discussing Ohio State's closer-than-expected 17-10 win at Illinois the day before.

Gonzalez, who had suffered a mild concussion the previous week against Minnesota and had practiced on a limited basis leading up to Illinois, had apparently misread a coverage against the Illini defense and, in layman's terms, had zigged when he should have zagged.

Tressel, seated behind his desk in his office at the Woody Hayes Athletics Center, was asking what happened.

"I need the practice," said Gonzo, as he is known to his teammates and coaches. "Quinn [Pitcock] and I were talking about that earlier today, and decided both of us are the types of players who need to practice in order to be at our best."

Pitcock suffered a concussion against Indiana two weeks earlier and sat out the Minnesota game. He returned to action against Illinois, but clearly was not up to snuff.

Both players were expected to be 100 percent for the upcoming trip to Northwestern, the final road game of the year for the Buckeyes.

Ten weeks into a grueling season, Ohio State had managed to stay remarkably healthy. Only Mike D'Andrea, who decided in the preseason to undergo another knee surgery, and Anderson Russell, who suffered a knee injury at Iowa, had been lost for the season. Heading in to the game at Northwestern, Alex Boone, the Buckeyes' massive left tackle, was the lone player listed as questionable. Had it been Michigan week, he would have played.

The close call at Illinois had the Buckeye Nation on edge. That game had been too close for comfort, especially with the all-important game with Michigan drawing ever nearer.

But for the always calm and cool Tressel, it was business as usual during the week. He had seen some things he didn't like at Illinois. The last 20 minutes were atrocious. But his team had played fairly well the first 40 minutes and with a break or two could have blown the game open before halftime.

There was no need to panic. In typical Jim Tressel fashion, this team would go back to work and correct its mistakes.

Once classes start in late September, the Buckeyes meet on Sunday to review the previous day's game and then take Monday off. The coaches, of course, are busy game-planning on Monday, mapping out the schedule for the entire week.

On this particular Monday, Tressel received some good news. Antonio Smith had been selected as one of 11 semifinalists for the Jim Thorpe Award and Pitcock had been selected as a finalist for the Lombardi Award.

The Thorpe Award goes to the best defensive back in college football and the Lombardi to the best player who lines up within five yards of the ball, meaning offensive and defensive linemen and linebackers are all eligible for the prestigious block of granite

Ohio State has had just one Thorpe Award winner over the years, Antoine Winfield in 1998. Six Buckeyes have won the Lombardi, including offensive tackle Orlando Pace in 1995 and '96 and linebacker A.J. Hawk last year.

Pitcock's selection as a finalist did not come as a surprise.

Ohio State's Brandon Mitchell runs for the end zone after intercepting a pass against Northwestern on November 11, 2006 in Evanston, Illinois.

With the Buckeyes in control of the game at Northwestern early, it was time for OSU fans to focus on the next order of business.

A three-year starter and one of this year's defensive co-captains, he came into the season recognized as one of the top defensive tackles in the country. The Piqua, Ohio, native is tough as iron and twice as strong.

Smith, on the other hand, qualifies as one of this year's true Cinderella's stories. A walk-on in 2002 and now a fifth-year senior, he had spent most of the past three seasons with the special teams. An outstanding student who is majoring in mechanical engineering, Smith was originally on an academic scholarship before being converted to athletic aid at the end of last year's Spring Practice.

At his end-of-the-year meeting with Tressel in the spring (the coach meets with all the players individually prior to the end of school), he had been asked if there was anything else on his mind.

"I'd really like to be included in the John Madden video game," he said. "But in order to do that, you need to be listed as a starter on the depth chart coming out of spring ball."

With the cornerback position opposite Malcolm Jenkins wide open, Tressel took the hint and graciously agreed to

Buckeyes running back Antonio Pittman rushes for some of his 80 yards on the day at Northwestern on November 11, 2006.

pencil in Smith at the No. 1 spot, all but guaranteeing him a place in X-Box history.

Smith responded by winning the starting job in fall camp and then getting better and better with each game. Against Penn State, and on national TV, he sealed the Buckeyes' victory with a fourth-quarter, 55-yard interception return for a touchdown. Against Indiana, he had a career high 12 tackles, including four tackles for loss and a 10-yard sack, and was named Big Ten co-defensive player of the week.

Now he had been tabbed as a semi-finalist for the Thorpe Award and no one could be more deserving.

On the heels of his selection for the Lombardi Award, Pitcock learned on Wednesday that he also was a finalist for the Lott Award, a relatively new award named for former San Francisco 49ers standout Ronnie Lott and based upon leadership, character and community involvement.

On Thursday, sophomore linebacker James Laurinaitis joined Penn State's Paul Posluszny and Mississippi's Patrick Willis as finalists for the Butkus Award.

If he wins the Butkus, Laurinaitis, who has led the team in tackles since the second week of the season and coming into this game was tied for the Big Ten lead in interceptions with five, would be just the second Ohio State player to do so. Andy Katzenmoyer won it as a sophomore in 1997. Chris Spielman was a two-time finalist in 1985 and '86 and Hawk was a finalist last year when Posluszny won it.

Two more short lists were announced on Thursday: Troy Smith was a finalist for the Davey O'Brien Quarterback Award and Joel Penton had been selected as a finalist for the Wuerffel Award, which like the Lott Award is based on character and community service. Penton, who plans to go into ministry work and, in fact, is already actively involved in that area, appeared to be a very strong contender for the latter honor.

After what Tressel described as a good week of practice, the Buckeyes headed to Evanston, Illinois on Friday, but not without a delay.

The Miami Air charter scheduled to take the team to Chicago had been backed into by a truck prior to the team arriving at Rickenbacker Airport. The charter company would have to fly in another plane and the scheduled 3:30 p.m. takeoff would be delayed.

The second plane arrived around 4:15 and the team boarded the aircraft about 45 minutes later. Unfortunately, just about that time, a series of storms was sweeping across Illinois and the air traffic controllers instructed Buckeye One to sit tight.

At about 8:15 p.m., the pilot received permission to take off. Weather was still an issue, however, as vicious thunderstorms lashed Chicago forcing both O'Hare Field and Midway Airport to close. The flight was then diverted to Billy Mitchell Field in Milwaukee, where the team boarded buses for the hour-long ride to the team hotel. The Friday night team meal, which always includes pecan rolls from the Ohio State golf course (a tradition started by former coach Woody Hayes), was served at about 10:30 p.m. local time and the players went to their rooms to get some much-needed rest.

It had been a long day, but no one complained. There was a football game to play the next day. With the Michigan game a week away, the coaching staff had hoped to play the early game on Saturday. As it turned out, the 2:30 p.m. kick-off against the Wildcats was a good thing.

Much of the banter in the press box on Saturday revolved around Ohio State's travel woes on Friday and whether or not that kind of distraction would cause the Buckeyes to lose some of their intensity.

That question was answered quickly as the Buckeyes jumped out to a 21-0 lead with 3:38 to play in the first quarter. All three OSU touchdowns followed Northwestern turnovers.

First, Laurinaitis forced a fumble that was recovered by Brandon Mitchell at the Ohio State 45-yard line. Five plays later the Buckeyes had a 7-0 lead as Smith hit Brian Hartline

Ohio State quarterback Troy Smith unloads one of his 19 passes against the Wildcats, 11 of which he completed, four of which were caught for touchdowns.

for a 14-yard score. It was the first career touchdown for Hartline, a redshirt freshman from North Canton, Ohio.

On Northwestern's next possession, Antonio Smith recovered a C.J. Bacher fumble at the Northwestern 27. It took the Buckeyes all of 84 seconds to score again with tailback Antonio Pittman scoring on a one-yard run.

The lead ballooned to three touchdowns on a 46-yard interception return by Mitchell. The Buckeyes had run just 13 plays and had a 21-0 lead.

Mitchell's interception was his second of the year and continued the defense's string of at least one interception in every game. The Ohio State defense now had 25 takeaways compared to 12 all of last year. Equally amazing, the Buckeyes had converted those turnovers into 114 points. By way of comparison, coming into the Northwestern game, the Ohio State offense had turned the ball over 11 times, but the opposition had not scored a point as a result of its good fortune.

After a Northwestern field goal, Ohio State took a 27-3 lead (the PAT was blocked) on a nine-yard pass from Smith to Hartline, who quickly doubled his career touchdown total. Larry Grant, a junior college transfer, set the table by blocking and recovering a Wildcat punt at the Northwestern 16-yard line. Three plays later, Smith found Hartline all alone in the back of the end zone.

Northwestern cut the Ohio State lead to 27-10 on an eight-yard pass from Bacher to tailback Tyrell Sutton. The drive covered 75 yards and took just six plays.

But any hopes of a Wildcats' comeback were dashed just before halftime when Smith threw his third touchdown pass of the day. Ted Ginn was on the receiving end of the 34-yard rainbow, catching the ball in his bread basket at the five and waltzing into the end zone with three seconds remaining in the half.

The Buckeyes added three more touchdowns, including Smith's fourth TD toss of the afternoon, and came up with two more turnovers in the second half to send Pat Fitzgerald's young team down to its eighth loss of the year.

The 54-10 final score had to be particularly difficult for the 33-year-old Fitzgerald, whose Wildcats had looked like world beaters the week before in a 21-7 win at Iowa.

In recording their highest point total since 1996, the Buckeyes rolled up 425 yards in total offense, including 231 yards rushing.

Pittman finished with 80 yards and topped the 1,000-yard mark for the second consecutive season, becoming the first OSU running back since Eddie George (1994-95) to enjoy back-to-back 1,000-yard seasons.

Freshman Beanie Wells enjoyed his best day, rushing for 99 yards and a touchdown and quarterback Todd Boeckman came off the bench to score his first career rushing touchdown.

Smith was named Big Ten co-offensive player of the week following his performance, his third four-touchdown game of the year passing.

The Buckeyes were 11-0 on the year and had stretched the nation's longest winning streak to 18 games. Only one other Ohio State team, Jim Tressel's 2002 national championship squad, had gone 12-0. All that stood in this team's way was next week's visitor—Michigan. ■

#1 Ohio State vs Northwestern (Nov 11 2006 at Evanston, Ill.)

Score by Quarters	1	2	3	4	Score	
Ohio State	21	12	14	7	54	Record: (11-0,7-0)
Northwestern	0	10	0	0	10	Record: (3-8,1-6)

OSU's Larry Grant smothers Northwestern punter Slade Larscheid's attempt during their Big Ten matchup in Evanston, Illinois.

That Team up North
Ohio State 42, Michigan 39

In a normal year, Michigan Week takes on a life of its own. The coaching staff is more intense, the players more attentive. Fans proudly wear their school colors to work and the oftentimes idle chitchat around the water cooler and in the lunch room turns exclusively to The Game. Members of the national media descend on Columbus in droves, eager to cover what most sports fans agree is the "Greatest Rivalry in Sports." Those 105,000 or so fans lucky enough to have a ticket to Ohio Stadium are the envy of football fanatics from coast-to-coast. For this one week, current events take a backseat to The Event.

All of that occurs in a normal year, and this is anything but! Much to the contrary, this year will be accorded a special place in the history of one of the most storied rivalries in college football.

To begin with, both teams took perfect 11-0 records into the game on November 18. Both were unbeaten in 1970 and again in 1973, but never before have two Big Ten teams owned spotless 11-0 records.

This also was the first time the Ohio State-Michigan game has pitted a No. 1 team against a No. 2 team. There have been numerous 1 vs. 5, 3 vs. 4, 5 vs. 9 and other assorted top 10 match-ups between the two, but never a 1 vs. 2.

And never in the relatively brief history of the Bowl Championship Series have both teams been in the picture for the National Championship Game. To the winner would go all the spoils.

In the Ohio State camp, preparation is intense. Interviews are shut off after Monday allowing the players to focus on the task at hand and lessening the risk of any inflammatory quotes that might make their way to the Michigan locker room. Motivational signs are plastered throughout the Woody Hayes Athletics Center. Practices are closed. Security is tight.

At Monday's press luncheon, Buckeye coach Jim Tressel met with the media for about 30 minutes, first talking about Michigan and then fielding questions from an overflow crowd of scribes and radio and TV reporters from around the country. Usually, between 50 and 60 members of the media attend the event. There were well over a hundred present this week.

Tressel routinely begins the session by reviewing the previous week's game. Not this time.

"I suppose I should have mentioned last week's game, but we haven't thought much about it," he said with a sheepish grin. "Just being honest."

Following the coach's interview, the media moved to the Woody Hayes Athletics Center (WHAC for short) to interview five offensive and five defensive players. Each group would be available for 45 minutes, first the offense and then the defense. Even figuring in a little extra time for the networks (ESPN and ABC) to do their interviews, all media requirements for the week would be wrapped up by 3 p.m.

During Michigan Week, interviews are limited to seniors and players who have played in the game. Troy Smith, Doug Datish, T.J. Downing, Antonio Pittman, and Anthony Gonzalez represented the offense; while Quinn Pitcock,

Jamie Sabau

Freshman tailback Chris Wells breaks free for a 52-yard touchdown run in the second quarter.

David Patterson, Jay Richardson, Antonio Smith, and Brandon Mitchell carried the defensive standard. All but Pittman and Gonzalez are seniors. Not surprising if you have followed Jim Tressel during his stay at Ohio State. Whenever possible he prefers his seniors to be the spokesmen.

Smith, of course, drew the most attention. The veteran quarterback, surrounded by a horde of tape recorders and cameras, fielded each question with the same poise that he exhibits on the field, always flashing his engaging smile. The other nine players also received their fair share of attention and did well. They had given the media plenty to write about.

On Wednesday, the Athletics Communications Office received word that Smith and Pitcock had been named to first-team berths on the American Football Coaches Association (AFCA) All-America team, and sophomore linebacker James Laurinaitis was a first-team selection on the Football Writers Association of America (FWAA) defensive team (the offensive team would be selected the next week). Neither squad would be announced until after Thanksgiving, so the coaching staff would not inform the players of their selection until after Saturday's game. Individual honors come at the end of the season.

Shortly after noon on Friday, coach Jim Tressel received the saddening news that former Michigan coach Bo Schembechler had passed away earlier that morning. There would be a moment of silence the next day for Bo, who was a native Ohioan and had coached under Woody Hayes from 1958 to 1962 before going on to become the winningest coach in Michigan football history.

"Bo was an extraordinary man and coach," said Tressel. "He was both a Buckeye and a Wolverine. Our thoughts and prayers are with everyone who grieves his loss."

Early that evening, following their customary Friday night meal at the Ohio State Golf Course, the team and coaches settled in at the Blackwell Inn just 300 or so yards from Ohio Stadium. Saturday could not get here soon enough.

The early week forecast for Saturday had called for rain and maybe even some snow. But, while it was overcast in the morning, there was no sign of any type of precipitation, a fact that could work in the Buckeyes' favor.

ESPN GameDay and GameDay Radio were set up in their usual locations south of St. John Arena, and by 9:30 a.m. the crowd of more than 2,500 was in a frenzy, waiting to hear the predictions of Lee Corso and Kirk Herbstreit. If Corso knew what was good for him, the veteran coach turned showman would put on a Brutus head when he made his pick.

More than 1,100 media credentials had been given out for the game, including one to a writer from Tokyo. The list from around the country was equally impressive with the Los Angeles Times, the San Diego Union-Tribune, the Austin-American Statesman, the Houston Chronicle, the San Antonio Express, the Dallas Morning News, the Arizona Republic, the Denver Post, the Atlanta Constitution, the Miami Herald, the St. Louis Post-Dispatch, the Chicago Tribune, the Chicago Sun-Times, the Washington Post, the New York Times, the New York Daily News, the New York Post, the Boston Globe, the Kansas City Star and USA Today all in attendance, along with HBO, ESPN The Magazine and a number of prominent dot.com entities. Representatives from the BCS, the Fiesta, Sugar, Orange and Rose Bowls were also on hand. It is hard to imagine a game drawing more attention.

The press box was full and the sidelines were jammed, mostly with media, but also with an occasional celebrity such as Eddie George, Derek Jeter and the award winning country-western group Rascal Flatts. It this wasn't the national championship game, it was the next best thing. And for Ohio State fans it was more important anyway.

To them, this was more than extending the Buckeyes' 18-game winning streak or becoming the fifth team ever to win two 1 vs. 2 showdowns in the same year. This was more important than being rated No. 1 from wire to wire

Ted Ginn Jr. spins away from Michigan's Morgan Trent for extra yardage after a catch.

Antonio Pittman rumbled for
139 yards against Michigan.

or capturing the school's first outright Big Ten championship since 1984. This was about beating Michigan and little else mattered.

Over the years, Ohio State has played in a number of big games. Every Michigan game is important. The 1969 Rose Bowl, and subsequent National Championship, was huge. The two-game series with Notre Dame in 1995 and '96 focused the national spotlight on the Buckeyes. So did the Texas games the past two years. But in the 116 years since Ohio State first began fielding a football team, this was shaping up as the most important game ever played by the Buckeyes.

Prior to the game, the team walked from the hotel to St. John Arena for the skull session, where more than 13,000 fans gather before each game to hear the Ohio State Marching Band rehearse its pre-game and halftime show.

As the team made its way down the southeast ramp and on to the floor there was a deafening roar. Then silence, as first a senior and then the coach offered a few thoughts. The ovation that Tressel received was extremely moving. This is a man who can do no wrong in the eyes of the Buckeye faithful.

"This is the day," he said with a raspy voice the result of a sore throat that had been bothering him the latter part of the week. "Our seniors are the best. Go Bucks!"

As coach Woody Hayes used to say, "All the hay is in the barn" at this point. All that was left to do now was to play the game.

Both teams came into the game with impressive numbers. Ohio State led the Big Ten in scoring offense at 35.8 points per game and led the nation in scoring defense at 7.8 points per game. Michigan led the Big Ten in total defense, giving up just 231.5 yards per game and was No. 1 in the conference against the run, allowing just 29.9 yards per game.

Ohio State had the home-field advantage and was considered a slight favorite. Most of the experts were predicting a low-scoring game that would go right down to the wire. Well, at least they got the last part of the equation right.

Former Ohio State and NFL standout Paul Warfield was the Buckeyes' honorary captain for the day. He accompanied the team captains to midfield and was given the honor of flipping the coin. Michigan called heads. It came up tails. Game on!

Michigan took a quick 7-0 lead, going 80 yards in seven plays with relative ease on its first possession. Junior quarterback Chad Henne was perfect on four passes, three of which went to wide receiver Mario Manningham, moving his team inside the OSU 1-yard line in six plays. Tailback Mike Hart scored around right end on the next play. The Buckeyes would have to come from behind.

Smith immediately went to work and took his team down the field for the tying touchdown, a 1-yard pass to Roy Hall in the right corner of the end zone and almost directly in front of the Michigan cheering section. The Buckeyes converted four third-down plays on the 69-yard drive, including three completions to Hall, one of which was on third-and-16.

The track meet was on.

The Buckeyes took a 14-7 lead early in the second quarter on a 52-yard run by freshman tailback Beanie Wells, who had come in to give starter Antonio Pittman a breather. It was the longest run of the year for Wells, who was hit in the backfield, but spun a way from the tackler and then burst to daylight through a gaping hole on the right side. The two-play, 58-yard drive took all of 57 seconds.

The Buckeyes forced Michigan to punt on its next possession and Ted Ginn Jr. called for a fair catch at his own 9-yard line. On second-and-six, Smith made another one of his patented Heisman moves, somehow eluding the on-coming rush and then spinning out of trouble and finding Brian Robiskie for a 39-yard pick-up.

Robiskie, the son of Cleveland Browns' assistant coach

Jamie Sabau

Ted Ginn Jr. hauls in a 39-yard touchdown pass in the second quarter.

Terry Robiskie, made a nice catch on the sideline, spun out of trouble himself and almost went the distance before being tripped up just past midfield. After a nine-yard gain by Pittman, Smith faked to Wells on a dive play and then went up top to Ginn who caught the ball between two defenders. The Buckeyes had gone 91 yards in four plays and led 21-7.

"We hoped we might catch them thinking we were going for the first down," said Tressel.

Michigan responded with an impressive 80-yard march of its own to cut the deficit to 21-14 with 2:28 to play. Hart moved the ball to midfield with a 30-yard run and four plays later Henne and Adrian Arrington hooked up on a 37-yard touchdown on which Arrington slipped two tackles on his way to the end zone.

Michigan appeared to have regained the momentum, but Ohio State had other ideas.

Taking over at their own 20-yard line, the Buckeyes executed their two-minute offense to perfection, marching smartly down the field on a nine-play, 80-yard scoring drive. Smith hit nine of 10 passes on the drive, the last of those an 8-yard scoring strike to Anthony Gonzalez on a slant with just 20 seconds left.

Ohio State led 28-14 at the half and had 320 yards in total offense. Smith had completed 21 of 26 passes for 241 yards and three touchdowns. His TD pass to Gonzalez, who is almost unstoppable on the slant, was his 29th touchdown pass of the year, tying the school single-season record originally set by Bobby Hoying in 1995. The Buckeyes also had rushed for 79 yards on 10 carries against the Wolverines' stout run defense.

Ohio State would get the ball to start the second half and a quick score may have put the game out of reach. Instead, the Buckeyes were forced to punt and Michigan took over on its own 40.

Just as they had done to open the game, the Wolverines struck quickly, moving 60 yards in five plays for their third touchdown of the day, which was one more than any of the Buckeyes' first 11 opponents had managed.

Hart carried the ball on the last four plays of the drive, picking up 8, 33, 16 and 2 yards, the last one for the score.

All of a sudden it was a seven-point ball game.

In his previous two starts against Michigan, Smith had not turned the ball over. That streak came to an end on the Buckeyes' next possession, when Alan Branch grabbed a deflected pass at the Ohio State 25-yard line. Smith was looking for Robiskie on the play, but Robiskie was popped by a pair of Michigan defenders just as the ball got there and the ball bounced into the air and into Branch's hands.

But after Hart picked up five yards, he was dropped for a two-yard loss by Laurinaitis. Henne then misfired on third down and Michigan had to settle for a 39-yard field goal by Garrett Rivas. The Wolverines had cut the deficit to 28-24, but had not scored a touchdown. The Buckeyes' defensive stand on that series would turn out to be the difference in the game.

Again, the Buckeyes answered. This time it was Pittman, who burst through a gaping hole on the right side courtesy of Steve Rehring and T.J. Downing and raced 56 yards for his 13th touchdown of the season. This time, the two-play, 65-yard drive took 37 seconds.

"I don't think anyone laid a glove on him," Tressel said afterwards during the post-game press conference.

It was 35-24 and the Buckeyes had some breathing room.

But strange things happen in Ohio State-Michigan games, and just before the end of the third quarter the Wolverines recovered an errant snap from center at the Buckeyes' 25 yard line. Hart's third touchdown made it 35-31 with 14:30 to play in the game.

The Wolverines had scored 10 points off two Ohio State miscues. Coming into the game, the Buckeyes had committed 13 turnovers on the season, but had not given up a single point. The Ohio State offense, meanwhile, had scored 127 points off 27 opponent turnovers.

James Laurinaitis (33) and Antonio Smith (14) pressure Chad Henne in the backfield and force a penalty for intentional grounding early in the game.

The Buckeyes then took over at their own 26 and moved the ball to the Michigan 28 before fumbling for the second consecutive series when the center snap hit a divot and dribbled into the OSU backfield, where it was recovered by the Wolverines' LaMarr Woodley. The normally efficient OSU offense had squandered a key opportunity to widen the lead.

After a Michigan punt, the Buckeyes got the ball back at their own 17-yard line and this time they were not to be denied as Smith marched his team toward the south stands and delivered a 13-yard scoring strike to Robiskie, who just managed to get his foot down before falling out of bounds. The play was reviewed, but upheld, and the Buckeyes had a 42-31 lead with 5:38 to play and Smith had his fourth touchdown pass of the day and undisputed possession of the school single-season record.

Michigan wasn't about to concede. The Buckeyes had gone 83 yards in 11 plays and the Wolverines responded by going 81 yards in 11 plays to cut the lead to 42-37. Henne hit eight of 11 passes on the drive, the last of which was a 16-yard scoring toss to tight end Tyler Ecker. The two-point conversion made it a three-point ballgame.

The record crowd of 105,708 was on its feet for the ensuing on-side kick. Ginn, who had enjoyed a monster day with eight receptions for 104 yards, fielded the ball at the Michigan 48 for his most important grab of the day.

A glance at the scoreboard showed 2:16 remaining on the clock. Michigan was out of timeouts, but the Buckeyes needed a first down to guarantee the Wolverines did not get the ball back. The always dependable Pittman picked up nine yards on the first play. On third-and-two, his six yard run to the Michigan 34 moved the chains. The Buckeyes would not need to run another play. The game was over.

Ohio State finished with 503 yards in total offense, including 187 yards rushing. Smith threw for 316 yards and rushed for 12 more, giving him 1,051 yards in total offense in his three games against Michigan. Pittman ran for 139 yards and averaged 7.7 yards per carry. The OSU defense was led by Laurinaitis with 9 tackles and had four sacks. The Ohio State offensive line, it should be noted, surrendered just one sack.

With the win, Smith becomes just the second Ohio State quarterback to lead the Buckeyes to three consecutive wins over the Wolverines. The first, now 91-year-old Tippy Dye, met Smith on Friday and was in attendance at the game.

At the skull session, Smith told the crowd, "I have been at this university for five years. I came here as a boy. I leave here as a man."

Actually, he leaves here as The Man!

The Buckeyes had won the outright Big Ten title. There would be a new picture hanging in the remodeled Woody Hayes Athletics Center. Maybe two. Only time would tell. ▪

#2 Michigan vs #1 Ohio State (Nov 18, 2006 at Columbus, Ohio)

Score by Quarters	1	2	3	4	Score	
Michigan	7	7	10	15	39	Record: (11-1,7-1)
Ohio State	7	21	7	7	42	Record: (12-0,8-0)

Ohio State set an attendance record with more than 105,000 fans in the historic No. 1 vs. No. 2 match up against Michigan.

David Patterson closes in on Michigan quarterback Chad Henne.

Just One Agenda

Every once-in-awhile, a special collection of athletes comes along; a group that is totally unselfish and committed to one another and the team concept. The 2006 Ohio State football team is just such a group.

Led by 19 amazing seniors, 18 of whom are in their fifth years, the Buckeyes have dedicated themselves to perfection. After twelve games, they are one game away from achieving that goal.

Starting with a 35-14 win over visiting Northern Illinois in the season opener, the Buckeyes have methodically rolled over one opponent after another en route to an unblemished 12-0 record.

Along the way, they survived a brutal September that included road games with Texas and Iowa and a home game with defending Big Ten co-champion Penn State.

In October, Ohio State had to go on the road and beat a reeling, but ever-dangerous, Michigan State team that too often had played the role of spoiler for the Buckeyes.

The month of November included less-than-smooth road trips in terms of travel to Illinois and Northwestern and the always emotional and difficult match-up with arch-rival Michigan.

Throughout the season this team has been undeterred in reaching its objective, and now they are one game away from Ohio State's second national championship in the last five years.

Much of the credit goes to this year's captains—quarterback Troy Smith, center Doug Datish and defensive tackles Quinn Pitcock and David Patterson. They have done a tremendous job of keeping this team focused.

But seniors T.J. Downing, Tim Schafer, Stan White, Jay Richardson, Joel Penton, John Kerr, Antonio Smith and Brandon Mitchell all have taken an active leadership role and deserve credit for what they have meant to the chemistry of this team.

There are no individuals on this team. The seniors have seen to that.

Of course, it is the coaching staff, led by head coach Jim Tressel, who has molded this group of young men and given it the character it needed to survive 12 straight grueling weeks of football. Tressel is indeed an amazing coach. He is even more amazing as a man, and his assistants all have his same high values and ethical standards.

Ohio State has won seven national championships over the years. Whether or not No. 8 is in the immediate future remains to be seen. But with 51 days to prepare for the next opponent, whoever that might be, you have to like the Buckeyes' chances. Given that amount of time to get ready, Tressel is a master.

No matter what happens, the 2006 Buckeyes are the undisputed Big Ten champions. They did it with Just One Agenda. ■

Heisman Trophy candidate Troy Smith kept the team focused throughout the big game with Michigan.

2006 Ohio State Football

Ohio State Game Results (as of Nov. 18, 2006)
All Games

Date	Opponent	Score	Overall Record	Conference Record	Time	Attend
Sep 2, 2006	NORTHERN ILLINOIS	W 35-12	1- 0- 0	0- 0- 0	2:51	103896
Sep 09, 2006	at #2 Texas	W 24-7	2- 0- 0	0- 0- 0	3:06	89422
Sep 16, 2006	CINCINNATI	W 37-7	3- 0- 0	0- 0- 0	3:03	105037
* Sep 23, 2006	#24 PENN STATE	W 28-6	4- 0- 0	1- 0- 0	2:53	105266
* Sep. 30 2006	at #13 Iowa	W 38-17	5- 0- 0	2- 0- 0	3:07	70585
Oct 7, 2006	BOWLING GREEN	W 35-7	6- 0- 0	2- 0- 0	2:51	105057
* Oct 14, 2006	at Michigan State	W 38-7	7- 0- 0	3- 0- 0	3:04	73498
* Oct 21, 2006	INDIANA	W 44-3	8- 0- 0	4- 0- 0	2:59	105267
* Oct 28, 2006	MINNESOTA	W 44-0	9- 0- 0	5- 0- 0	2:50	105443
* Nov 04, 2006	at Illinois	W 17-10	10- 0- 0	6- 0- 0	3:00	53351
* Nov 11 2006	at Northwestern	W 54-10	11- 0- 0	7- 0- 0	2:57	47130
* Nov 18, 2006	#2 MICHIGAN	W 42-39	12- 0- 0	8- 0- 0	3:28	105708

Ohio State fans hold up newspapers after the Buckeyes' memorable victory over Michigan on November 18, 2006 in Columbus.

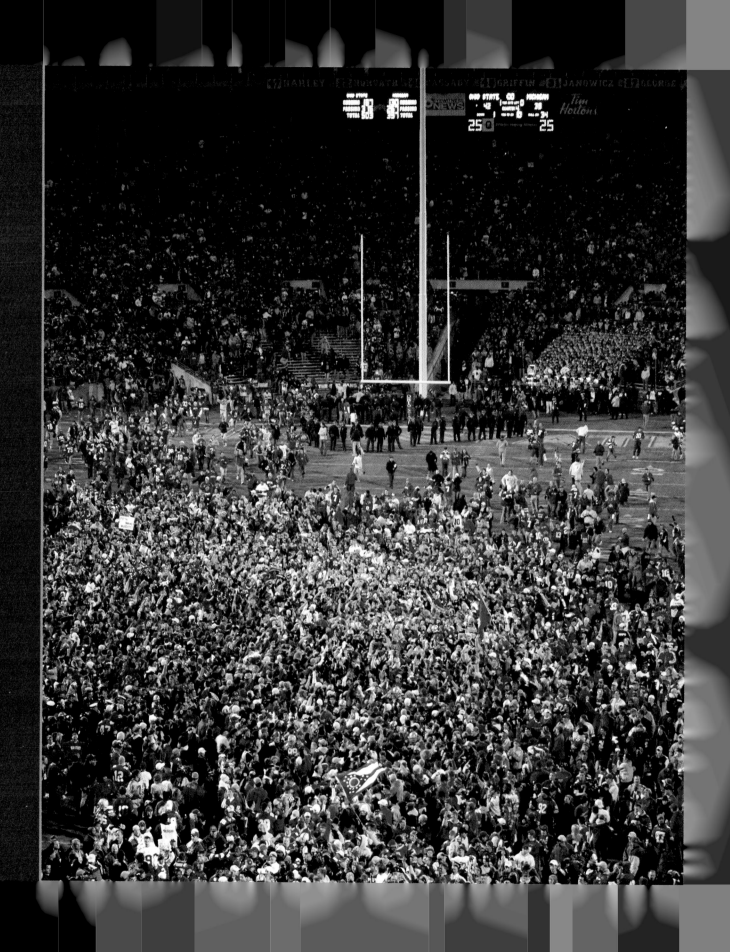